THE EVADED DUTY

"Nulli vendemus, nulli negabimus
aut differemus, rectum aut
justitiam."

"To no man will we sell, or deny, or
delay, right or justice."

Magna Carta 1215

"Every state has the duty to promote,
through joint and separate action,
realisation of the principle of
equal rights and self-determination
of peoples . . . . "

Resolution No. 2625 (XXV)
General Assembly, United Nations
24 October 1970.

D1453837

THE
EVADED DUTY

LOUIS FITZGIBBON

REX COLLINGS

LONDON
1985

First published in the United Kingdom by
Rex Collins Ltd, 6 Paddington Street, London W1

© Louis FitzGibbon 1985

Typeset by Tellgate Ltd, London WC1
Printed and bound in Great Britain by
Biddles Ltd, Guildford and King's Lynn

FitzGibbon, Louis
  The evaded duty.
  1. Somalia—Boundaries   2. Somalia—History
  I. Title
  911'.6773   DT403.3

  ISBN 0-86036-209-4

DEDICATION

This book is dedicated to the concept of Justice, and to those who fight for its achievement in Western Somalia.

Above all, this book is not concerned with poetry.
The subject of it is War, and the Pity of war.
The Poetry is in the Pity.

Wilfred Owen 1893-1918
Poems (1920) Preface.

It is also dedicated to those, as yet unknown, who, having read what is herein written, will be fired by determination and make it their business that Justice shall be done.

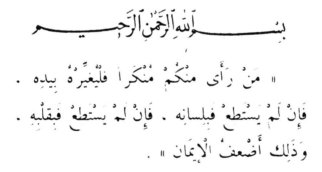

Whosoever of you sees an evil action, let him change it with his hand; and if he is not able to do so, then with his tongue; and if he is not able to do so, then with his heart and that is the weakest of faith.

Contents

Acknowledgement

The author offers profound gratitude to the many who, in their several ways, have helped him to compile the facts which have inspired the purpose of this work.

They are too numerous to name and, in any case, such a catalogue implies an order of precedence which would be highly unbecoming in that all are equal in their contributions.

They know themselves, and the author thanks them all.

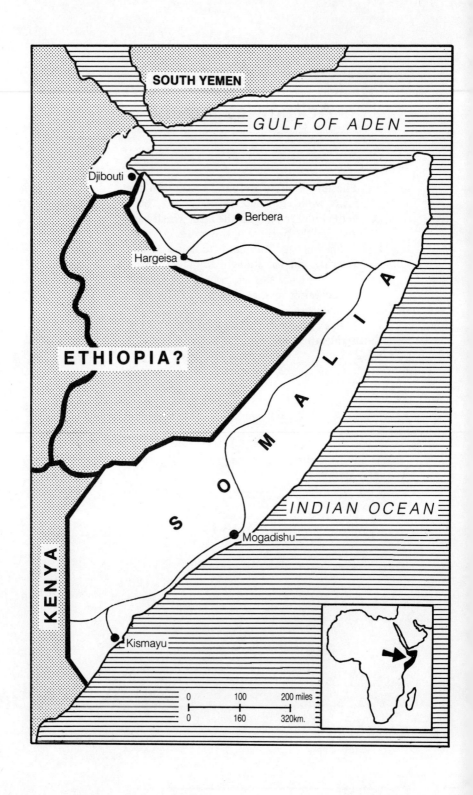

Preface

Deep in the throbbing heart of Africa there are many wounds. Some have healed, others become less painful with the relief of progress, but there remain a few which continue to bleed and call for remedy. One such is the plight of the Somalis in Ethiopia, as they struggle against a malignant black colonialism which has lasted nearly one hundred years. Like some vile pestilence, this domination brings only torture, mutilation and death; from it flows an anguished stream of refugees who leave behind the bodies of their relatives – remains which are hidden from public notice by a catafalque of international indifference. Yet these wretched Somalis have a right every bit as human as that enjoyed elsewhere – the right to self-determination, the realisation of which it is the duty of the nations to ensure.

Despite the U.N. principles of which we hear so much, *that duty has been evaded*.

It is proper at once to say that this work deals exclusively with these imprisoned Somalis, and the right which they have been denied, although the peoples of Eritrea, Tigray and Oromia are in the same *oubliette* and suffer the same torment. Great advances have been made in education and general knowledge, but there remains considerable ignorance of both Somalia and Ethiopia so that some brief explanation is required as a necessary background. In so far as this work is concerned with action at international level, mention must be made of the United Nations and of the European Community as represented by the European Parliament for this is not just a matter for today but also for tomorrow.

My subject has been included in several books and treatises, but usually only as part of a larger exposition. It is, however, one of such magnitude and so basic to merit a new revelation in which it is the central theme. In this way it may attract the attention it so richly deserves uncluttered by other considerations. It is a theme long the victim of a cover-up brought about by misrepresentation, fear of antagonism, hostile propaganda and lack of a voice strong enough to reach the ears of the human family. But to hide a scandal is not to cause it to vanish; rather it exacerbates it by adding the affront of disregard. Furthermore, while laudable efforts have and are being made to help refugees, the root causes of their flight is something from which the nations have turned their heads in a way reminiscent of Winston Churchill's comment on the Katyn massacre: 'The issue should be avoided'.

It is hardly possible for a single individual to attempt to promote a cause of this size; all he can do, within the limits of his capability, is to draw attention to it in the hope that his argument may find its way to the proper forum where it can be examined to a point where some action is taken. That, quite simply, is the objective of this work in the name, of Justice.

For those who may indeed wish to take the case further, the road will be arduous: there will be weighty objections, numerous excuses, gerrymandering of records and much pressure overt or subvert. There may even be personal risk, but in the belief that justice will prevail, something must be done irrespective of the success or failure which may attend the start – for if no such effort is made, then humanity condemns itself by its own tongue, and will risk being gripped by the rage of Caliban.

It is my conviction that here is a problem fundamental to the essence of humanity, and delay in approaching it should not be understood to mean that it is incapable of a just and proper solution – for if we are not part of a solution, then we are part of the problem.

Louis FitzGibbon

Chapter 1

THE SOMALIS

In my previous book: *The Betrayal of the Somalis* I devoted two chapters to these little-known people and their history. Some of what is now written will appear repetitive to those who have read my earlier work and to those who have read the far more authoritative books of Professor I.M. Lewis and others. However, to the newcomer to this subject some explanation must be given. Somalia forms that north-eastern tip of Africa where it juts out into the Indian Ocean, and its 3200 kilometers of coastline runs from the Bab-el-Mandeb (known as the southern gate of the Red Sea) eastwards along the gulf of Aden to Cape Gardafui, and then south-westwards along the Indian Ocean to Ras Kiamboni at the border with Kenya. Containing an area of some 640,000 sq.kms, Somalia is the size of France and Italy put together. The North of the country is mountainous, but the main part of the country consists of a plateau which rises slowly from the south to the Golis range; the range itself runs parallel to the north coast and boasts mountains rising to 8,000 ft. Between this range and the sea is a narrow plain known as 'guban' where temperatures reach extremes of heat. For the rest, the central part is a featureless savannah except between the only two rivers, the Shebelle and the Juba which contribute to the fertile Jubaland plain.

Somalia is mainly a hot dry country and the main object to greet the eye is the flat-topped acacia-thorn tree. By contrast, the far south-west between the Juba river and the boundary is enriched with forests in which wildlife abounds. The impression gained by a new arrival is of a vast shimmering plain endlessly stretching to almost invisible horizons under the infinite dome of the African sky. There is a sense of space perhaps only mirrored in the Sahara or in the white expanses of Siberia (to take but two examples). There is an impression of timelessness unknown in Europe and one feels that if one puts one's ear to the ground one may hear the deep beat of the heart of the world. Above all, there is freedom, silence and peace, as if one had stepped in at the moment when the world was first created, an impression heightened in

1

a way by the tall, hard and pointed ant-hills which rise in places to thrice the height of a man – like primeval giants standing still. Albeit created by living organisms, these pillars appear as if part of an enormous structure from which the roof has been removed. As to colour; it is a panorama of brownish-yellow which contrasts with the deep and pure blue of the dome above. Time stands still and the vista trembles in the heat. Nothing moves. Such is but a paltry attempt to paint a sketch of the main part of Somalia – hard but indescribably beautiful to those who value solitude.

The history of Somalia stretches back to the mists of time. Known as 'The Land of Punt' in Pharaonic history, there existed a close commercial relationship with the Egyptians which had its apex in the period of Queen Hatsep-Sut (about 1500 BC). To the Phoenicians, Somalia was also known as 'The Region of Incense', but the Romans dubbed it 'Terra Incognita'. Numerous ancient Greek and Roman chronicles tell of the coast with its trading centres, the best known of which is 'The Periplus of the Erythraen Sea' written somewhere about AD 40. Ptolemy confirmed what was then written in his 'Geography' so that from all this we gain a sense of far-reaching national existence; and the word 'national' is of the essence in that Somalia is not so much a country but a nation of people bound together by a single ethos.

The advent of Islam, which arrived through trade, brought a new *modus vivendi* to the Somalis who were, and are still, primarily nomads wandering at will with their camels across the seemingly limitless plains of their land. Before the partition of these people by Britain, Ethiopia, France and Italy at the end of the 19th century, the Muslim Somali formed a well-defined national entity which occupied the eastern section of The Horn of Africa from close to the Awash River beyond Dire Dawa and Djibouti to the north, to the Tana River in the south in what is now Kenya. Culturally, ethnically and historically the Somali people belong to the Hamitic/Cushitic group, and their closest neighbours and relatives are the Oromo and Borana Galla to the west and south together with the Afar to the north in Djibouti, both sets having similarities in language through grammar and vocabulary. Unlike the Galla, the Somali socio-political structure is based on kinship. What is certain is that a deep gulf separates them from the Semitic-speaking Amharas of the central Abyssinian (Ethiopian) highlands. A further essential difference is that while the Somali are Muslim, the Amharas are Christian, and these two differences of fundamental belief are the main vehicles of expressed nationalism for each race. Physically striking, the Somali are easily distinguishable by their thin bone-structure and long narrow heads while their facial characteristics proclaim their long-standing

2

connections with Arabia in which the Somali take great pride and have done since the 10th century. However, despite this adherence to Islam, Arabic did not dispel the Somali language which is spoken from Djibouti down to Garissa in the south. Within that language there is a division as to the people who inhabit the inter-riverine area, but it makes no great impact upon the mode of Somali speech in general. The nation of the Somalis is divided therefore into two groups, the Sab and the Samale, the first comprising the tribes of Digil and Rahanwein, and the far larger second encompassing the Irir, Hawiye, Isaq, Dir and Darod (see map). These are rather clans than tribes for within them there is an extremely complicated tribal system. Hence although seemingly divided by the clan structure, Somalis are also unified through the genealogical combinations into a single national family.

Distinguished and learned students of the anthropology of the Somalis have come to the inescapable conclusion that speaking the same language, sharing the same religion, culture, as well as social and political institutions, they form a nation, and in so far as they occupy a separate.geographical region, Somalia in its widest sense qualifies for nationhood. Just where a line can be drawn to the west clearly to mark a natural boundary is not so easy to trace with accuracy, and while the Somalis say that Somaliland stops where 'the camel stops' is poetic and delightful, it would not be sufficient for, say, The International Court of Justice.

Proud and erect, the Somalis are known as 'The Irish of Africa' in that they are extremely generous yet fierce and war-like simultaneously. Of penetrating gaze and easy manner, they are people to be reckoned with, as history has clearly revealed. The men are known as 'Waranleh' or spear-bearers and that title does not just refer to weapons, but to their inbuilt and soul-depth natural determination to defend their independence. Living the hard life of a nomad is a school which breeds sturdy men, and the previously-described expanse of their land gives them an inate sense of freedom which they are ready to defend with the last drop of their blood. Not for them placatory arguments; what is theirs is theirs, and each and every one of them knows this in his bones. Past wrongs are not forgotten, nor is the sense of unity abandoned. It is this which prompted the national flag, a single white five-pointed star upon a background of azure-blue. The blue was 'borrowed' from the flag of the United Nations, and the five points of the star represent, from top clockwise: Djibouti, ex-British Somaliland, Ex-Italian Somaliland, North-East Kenya and eastern Ethiopia (as it became through treachery on the part of those who had no right to give it away). To the West, that part of Ethiopia is known as the 'Ogaden'

3

from the name of a tribe which inhabits it, but to Somalis it is known as Western Somalia. Of those five points, it is this one which is unacceptable, the more so as Somalis feel for their brothers imprisoned in an alien land. Just as the Irish seek the unity of their island, and as the Poles seek their freedom, so do the Somalis search for a way in which their kith and kin can obtain freedom through the principle of self-determination which is the subject of this work. At this point it is important to repeat what the President of Somalia has so often said; that Somalia has no territorial aspirations on any of her neighbours, but she cannot and will not relinquish her demand that Somalis in Western Somalia be freed and direct their national life as they wish. In short, the Somalis are only too well aware of the nature of betrayal, and they cannot ever betray their brothers. Yet such has been hostile propaganda, plotting and the intervention of a superpower that few even want to listen to this plea for justice such as it upheld but not activated by international bodies. Hence an original injustice is perpetuated by those whose duty it should be to right this wrong.

THE SOMALIS

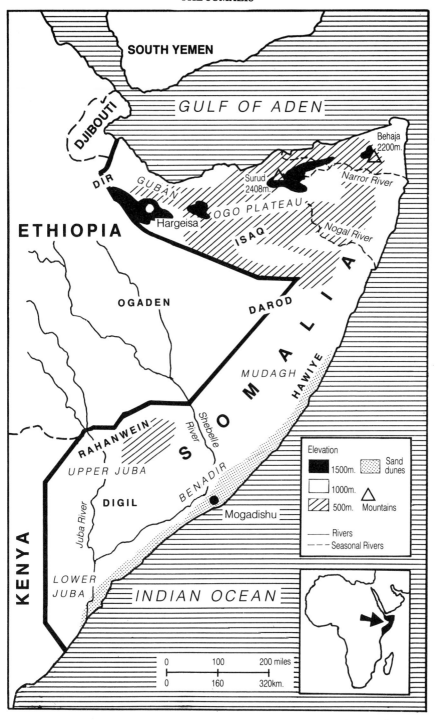

SOUTH YEMEN

DJIBOUTI

GULF OF ADEN

Behaja
2200m.

Surud
2408m.

Narror River

DIR

GUBAN

OGO PLATEAU

Hargeisa

Nogal River

ETHIOPIA

ISAQ

OGADEN

DAROD

SOMALIA

MUDAGH

HAWIYE

Shebelle River

RAHANWEIN

UPPER JUBA

BENADIR

DIGIL

Mogadishu

Juba River

KENYA

LOWER
JUBA

INDIAN OCEAN

Elevation

■ 1500m.

☐ 1000m.

▨ 500m.

▒ Sand dunes

△ Mountains

— Rivers

– – Seasonal Rivers

| 0 | 100 | 200 miles |
| 0 | 160 | 320km. |

Chapter 2

THE ETHIOPIAN ENIGMA

By contrast to the Somalis, as has been seen, the Abyssinians (or Ethiopians, as they have now become) are a totally different people who originate from the mountain fastness around Axum. Space does not permit a lengthy treatise upon Amharic history, but a clue can be found in the words of the late Emperor Haile Selassie who described his own country as 'a mystery'. How much more difficult, therefore, must it be for an outsider to plumb the depths of that State which abounds in contradictions and intricacies which even the Ethiopians do not comprehend. Historically labyrinthine, understanding of Abyssinia has been clouded by images it has itself projected for various reasons of gain or expansionism. The best card in the pack was the 'Christian' one played so adroitly by the Emperor Menelik (or King as he was originally). His famous statement that Ethiopia 'is a Christian Island in a Sea of Pagans' is now historic in that it gained for him the support of Christians in Europe for whom the very word 'pagan' was almost anathema. This last conjured up uneducated visions of sinister rites, of idolatry or even cannabalism inextricably mixed in which the conundrum of 'the dark continent' wherein so many intrepid explorers had lost their lives. Thus, in the European mind, there was a dread of the stygian gloom permeating a continent to which was applied the phrase 'white man's grave' and similar. True there were fascinations such as the mysterious Timbuktu and the source of the Nile, but generally Africa was a species of land to which the expression taboo best fitted. Little wonder, then, that Menelik's claim was seen as some kind of light; a godly beacon to which the well-intentioned swarmed like moths. It was in this way that Menelik was able to attract support both political and military seemingly to the Europeans for self-defence, but in reality to carry out a colonisation the results of which are excrutiatingly with us today. Further, Menelik was no fool, and he became adept in the art of manipulating his European friends through the differences which obtained amongst them, and in all of this he drew upon centuries-old Abyssinian experience of seeking foreign aid which stretched back to the 16th century.

Nor was that experience limited to cajoling and persuading; it also embraced the subtle ability to create propaganda, an ability unknown to his neighbours, especially the Somalis. Hence the Ethiopians increased their propensity for deception whether of others or even of themselves, and this faculty has been sharpened and tempered so that its use is even undetected in current political times and events. It is, in short, the secret weapon of the Ethiopians and is compounded by a guile of which few are suspicious.

As will be seen, Abyssinia, a hundred years ago was but a small kingdom limited to mountainous areas and so enclosed as to be unknown to the outside world and almost impenetrable even to those who sought to extend their knowledge. Except for the palace élite, it was a land of serfs within a feudal system of which sight had been lost to Europeans except in history-books. But the *realpolitik* of the Europeans last century placed in Menelik's hands the very tool he wanted to subdue his neighbours; the possession of firearms. In this the uprising of the Mahdi in the Sudan came to him as a blessing for he could link that movement of Islamic 'jehad' with the Muslims whom he sought to subdue – and he did so with unimaginable cruelty and as revenge for the progress of Ahmed Ibrahim Al Ghazi who, in 1533, so routed his Abyssinian adversaries that he came to control south and central Abyssinia.

Thus Abyssinia grew and grew and the capital moved ever southwards from Axum to Gondar and finally to Addis Ababa; with it also came the feudal system whereby the country was ruled by a handful of nobles and priests while the rest starved in penury and oppression. It was a system which continued until Haile Selassie was deposed in 1974, and subsequently murdered a year later. Within that time another figure arose, Benito Mussolini, and his attack upon Ethiopia in 1936 brought benefits to the Amharas in another way. The diminutive emperor fled to England where, by reason of the British love of royalty, he was welcomed with open arms. He was, as are many Ethiopians, 'charming' and the lion's mane with which he decorated his pith-helmet caught the imagination of the people. These people, too, were appalled by the Italian aerial-bombing of the Ethiopians which they saw as what would nowadays be called a 'war crime', albeit that they either did not know about or forgot that it had been the British who had aerially bombed Sayyid Mohamed Abdille Hassan at Taleh in North Somalia in the year 1920 – the man called 'The Mad Mullah of Somaliland' although he was neither mad nor mullah. Once an idea has taken root, or an individual clasped to the bosom of a host-nation, they become almost eradicable. Thus it is that the fantasy of Emperor Haile Selassie has lingered on in the British imagination and even reflected its false glow upon his successor, Colonel Mengistu Haile Mariam, better known in The Horn of Africa as the 'Red Emperor' by reason of his dependence upon the Soviets.

Additionally, the Abyssinians are by nature devious and clever at appearing as they wish to be seen. Suspicious of each other, they are doubly so of foreigners so that they take endless pains to study the foibles and backgrounds of any who are due to visit them in order that they may say what they consider wishes to be heard. To some they are indignant victims of interference in their internal affairs; to others they are humble supplicants of aid from the richer or more powerful. Thus they are able, as it were, to change their shape to suit their needs, which shape, of course, is overlaid with a thick sauce of apparent sincerity. In this cunning fashion they insinuate themselves (and their desires) into receptive but ill-informed hearts, and no opportunity of profit thereby is ever lost. This ability to act the chameleon is well known to the peoples of Eritrea, Tigray, Oromia, Sidamo and Western Somalia, but whatever warnings they utter are ignored.

Just as in 1969 Haile Selassie told lies about the famine, those lies were used by his enemies to depose him in 1974. The deposers, or Dergue (committee) were seen as deliverers by the multitudinous peoples of the Ethiopian empire who hoped that centuries of enslavement were about to end. They hoped in vain for Colonel Mengistu soon disposed of his competitors and there followed an horrific purging of enemies or supposed enemies which rightly became known as The Red Terror. This new regime took to itself the self-same prerogatives as had Haile Selassie, and it was into this maelstrom that the Soviets neatly stepped in 1977 when they proffered a hand gloved in friendship whereas the reality was no different from that which constantly tightens the thumbscrew on Poland, Afghanistan or any other country which has felt the deadly breath of Soviet communism.

The Human Rights record of the Ethiopian Dergue is so atrocious that even the unwilling have to acknowledge its existence, yet there is no international uproar such as there would be if, say, a single man were hanged in Central America. Droughts are not new in the Sahel, that broad belt which runs across Africa from Mauritania all the way to Somalia including Ethiopia; they are natural visitations caused by changes in the earth's climatic conditions. But famine is another thing; it can be an act of God or, on the other hand, it can be caused by man through indiscriminate bombing and burning of crops or by the impressment of farmers into an army and the consequent neglect of products necessary to nourish the common man. This latter factor is not even acknowledged as a possibility within international calculations of

8

aid to Ethiopia, and naturally, the Ethiopians keep it a secret. Thus here again we see a duplicity in the use of deliberate acts to attract the sympathy of others, and whereas no one wants not to help the starving, it is necessary to be sure that such help actually reaches those in need and is not used for other purposes such as feeding a huge army or paying a supplier for weapons of war. But what of the well-thumbed Christian card? Little is now heard of it for the reason that all religion is hateful to Soviet communism, and documents exist which set out specifically just how religion is to be rooted out.

In the face of the aforesaid record on human rights, present-day Ethiopia needs to create a better name for itself. To this purpose something humanitarian is required such as will bring in assistance and, at the same time, create friendlier relations whence even more aid can be expected. This is the explanation of the proliferating returnee and resettlement programmes announced by the Dergue about which so much is made.

In fact there are no voluntary returnees (as will be seen later) and the resettlement programmes are not as stated, but are carefully-planned methods of uprooting peoples from their natural habitat to a different place thereby causing confusion and depression which, in turn, dampen down the ardour to revolt. It is the same scheme whereby Estonians, Latvians and Lithuanians are removed from their countries and replaced by White Russians or other colonisers, and it amounts to a cruel psychological subterfuge to demoralise people to the point of despair. Similarly, Ethiopia claims to host millions of Sudanese refugees, and whereas there may be a few malcontents, the simple method of adding a nought or two to the figures appears to delude the United Nations and others, despite the fact that in-depth investigation is forbidden.

Resistance to the Dergue is not limited to Eritreans, the peoples of Tigray, Oromia, Sidamo or Western Somalia; even Amharas themselves bleed under the iron boot of this pitiless regime so that many of them have fled to Sudan. I went to Sudan in June of 1984 and met with representatives of no less than three such liberation fronts all struggling to cast out the Soviets, Cubans and others from Ethiopia and rid the country of the Dergue. Yet the Western media seem not to know of these hard-pressed people or, if they do, not to take any interest.

The enigma of Ethiopia therefore seems to be that it contains the seed not just of self-destruction, but that in its elimination of others by the most ferocious means, it escapes the universal condemnation it so richly deserves. The root of this puzzle seems to be the total unwillingness of others to read the truth however plainly spelled out. At the time of writing (summer 1984) we have yet to see what the new communist political party being foisted upon Ethiopia will do, but there are many indications that it will bind the Ethiopian regime even closer to the USSR as an instrument with which to extend Soviet expansionism further and further throughout Africa. Hence, from an isolated unknown and feudal state hidden away in mountains almost within living memory, Ethiopia has been transformed into a full satellite of one of the most evil conspiracies the world has ever seen. Freedom has eluded the Ethiopians and the Abyssinians from whom they came, and it appears now that they are prepared to sell themselves into deeper bondage while the West looks on benevolently and seemingly oblivious to such an obvious danger even to themselves. And why that should be so is another riddle.

Chapter 3

THE UNITED NATIONS

Many of the accomplishments of individual members of this Family of Nations merit sincere applause for in various ways they have brought benefits and amelioration of human suffering. The research and work of the World Health Organisation (WHO) is an example that springs to mind, and one could trace long lists of successes by UNDP, FAO, WFP, UNIDO, UNICEF, UNCTAD and ITU, to name but some.

Yet there are two chapters of UN history which are not so glorious. Given a trowel or a spade and a man may peacefully build a wall or dig a well; but when he has only a sword to use, his courage may well fail him. Again human nature is frail and prone to take the line of least resistance, neither can it always ignore self-interest. If that is true about an individual, so is it true of a body of men or an organisation of any kind, and this must be the more so in that committees or suchlike tend always to accept that which is not acrimonious so that the comfort of all can be accommodated. On 9 April 1981 the UN Commission on Human Rights appointed Prince Sadruddin Aga Khan as 'Special Rapporteur to study the question of human rights and massive exoduses'. No better choice of rapporteur could have been found in that Prince Sadruddin had, himself, been the UN High Commissioner for Refugees and thus would be able to draw upon a deep well of information and experience. He duly got to his task with both energy and determination and produced a heavy report for presentation at the Thirty-eighth session of the Commission on Human Rights which is part of the UN Economic and Social Council; it was numbered E/CN.4/1503 and dated 31 December 1981. It consisted of a letter of transmission, three chapters on conceptual framework; the relationship between Mass Exodus and violations of Human Rights and a Synopsis as well as Conclusions and Recommendations. It also contained three long annexes and an extensive bibliography, and it should be noted that whereas the first part (the introduction, three chapters, conclusions and recommendations) ran to 140 pages, the total of the annexes and the bibliography ran to a further 305 pages so that they formed over seventy-five percent of the whole, in fact they took up more than twice the number of total pages. Annex 2 contained four 'Case Studies' on Afghanistan, Ethiopia, Indo-China (Kampuchea, Lao People's Republic, Vietnam) and Mexico. They were all brutally honest and immediately a flurry ensued within the corridors of the United Nations. Under great pressure from the Ethiopian junta and the Soviet Union, the original report was withdrawn 'for technical reasons', and later appeared again shorn of all the annexes and the bibliography which contained no less than 414 valuable sources of information. It bore the same reference number and date but with a note attached indicating 're-issued for technical reasons'. There was no mention at all of the deleted material which, as has been shown, formed far the larger part of the whole report. Thus were the official records of the United Nations mutilated to cover-up the horrendous deeds committed by some of its own members. When I heard this I queried the reason for the deletions and was informed that it had been agreed in order to produce unanimous approval of the main part of the document. In so far as this work deals with the Horn of Africa, the case-study on Ethiopia which originally appeared in Annex II is reproduced as Appendix 1. It should be added that when the Somali Permanent Representative at the UN protested there were immediate and angry protests from the Ethiopians and, in the event, a key part of a formal report from the Secretary General's own Special Rapporteur was kept from the public eye. Mr Osman Saleh Sabbe, Chairman of the Central Council and Executive Committee of the Eritrean Liberation Front and People's Liberation Forces re-produced this part of Annex II in a leaflet entitled 'Suppressed!' but as the extent of his mailing list is not known, it is included here so that perhaps it may reach a wider public as a document which they have a right to see and study as being citizens of States which are members of the United Nations. The adulterated document E/CN.4/1503 duly appeared on the agenda, as item 12, of the thirty-eighth session of the Human Rights Commission dated 9 March 1982 (reference E/CN.4/1982/L.57) and the debate on it appears in the summary record of the 55th meeting of the 38th session of the Commission (reference E/CN.4/1982/SR.55 dated 26 March 1982), wherein pages 18 to 34 are relevant.

In para 80 on page 19 Prince Sadruddin said: 'The aim must be to seek speedy and effective ways of preventing the disastrous effects of large-scale population movements, since the cost of inaction soon might become unbearable.' The Canadian representative called for an examination of root causes and their removal, while the Australian representative declared that ' . . . the international community must face up to all aspects of the causes . . . '. Mr Salah-Bey (Algeria) stressed that root causes 'went beyond the personal ambitions of those in power to colonial origins . . . ' while Mrs Gu Yijie of China said that ' . . . the international community must therefore do its utmost to end this phenomenon.' She added, and this is of importance (as will be seen later) that 'exoduses . . . could only be settled through peaceful negotiations . . . including *safe* (author's emphasis) repatriation . . . ' Mrs Florez of Cuba also spoke of root causes, and then it came to the turn of Mr Terrefe of Ethiopia who (para 115, page 25) introduced the age-old and threadbare *caveat* that any solutions must have respect for the internal affairs of sovereign states. Mr Hilaly of Pakistan spoke of the 'denial of the right to self-determination' on two occasions, and this right was even referred to by Mr Chernenko of the USSR and by Mr Te Sun Hoa of Kampuchea. Winding up and in reply, Prince Sadruddin said, *inter alia*, ' . . . the causes had seldom received due attention.'

Here, then, is an example of the United Nations at work; an example of a debate on a document of which well over half had been removed beforehand, and a debate which paid only lip-service to both root causes of refugee flows and the right to self-determination. At the time of writing in Sudan and Somalia there were no less than 2 million refugees from Ethiopia, yet Ethiopia duly stood up to talk about a report partly decapitated by its mission and in full knowledge that the refugees of The Horn come from nowhere else than from its own country. As an exercises in hypocrisy it would be hard to beat, but even worse is to come.

Round about 1982 the United Nations began to prepare for and publicise the much-vaunted Second International Conference of Assistance to Refugees in Africa, and on 6 December in that year Ambassador Ahmed Mohamed Adan, the Somali Permanent Representative delivered a speech at the Third Committee on assistance to refugees. In that it refers to Prince Sadruddin's report and it is reproduced as Appendix 2. Such was the outburst it provoked from the Ethiopian representative that a right to reply was demanded and granted, the text of which appears as Appendix 3 and the contents of this reply are particularly appropriate to what follows, both as to ICARA II and to Djibouti.

The first International Conference on Assistance to Refugees in Africa (ICARA I) was not a great success, and thus it was felt that a second should be mounted. Despite what was said in New York and what I learned from private correspondence with the UK Permanent Representative in Geneva, it was apparent from the start that 'root causes' were not to be addressed by the Conference. Hence one can but come again to the sad conclusion that the UN pays only lip-service to its principles no matter how often they are trumpeted in debates and in publications. I attended ICARA II (9 to 11 July 1984) in Geneva, and it was

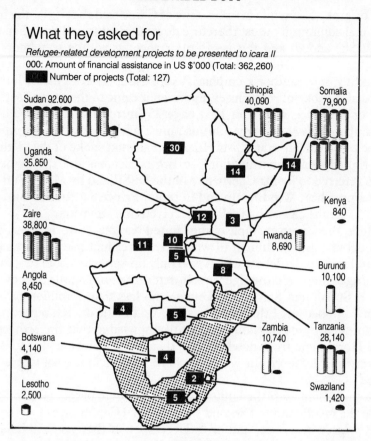

What they asked for

Refugee-related development projects to be presented to icara II
000: Amount of financial assistance in US $'000 (Total: 362,260)
◼ Number of projects (Total: 127)

Sudan 92.600

Ethiopia 40,090

Somalia 79,900

Uganda 35.850

30

14

14

Zaire 38,800

Kenya 840

12

3

11

10

5

Rwanda 8,690

Angola 8,450

8

Burundi 10,100

4

5

Botswana 4,140

4

Zambia 10,740

Tanzania 28,140

Lesotho 2,500

2

5

Swaziland 1,420

soon apparent that various states preferred to donate to Voluntary Agencies rather than to UNHCR as being more likely to get relief to the needy rather than have the UN give it to governments who actually exported refugees. Previously, however, on 9 February 1984 I had spoken to the senior UN representative in the UK, Mr Erik Jensen; it was not, therefore, a complete surprise that UNHCR and others evaded the basis of refugees, namely the root causes of their flight. Furthermore, Ethiopia asked for assistance with 70,000 refugees and 150,000 'returnees' which, as seen from Appendix 3 are highly dubious figures. Finally ICARA II provided evidence of the *refoulement* of refugees from Djibouti to Ethiopia which forms the subject of the rest of this chapter. The August issue of 'Development Report' issued by *The Economist* described ICARA II in a banner headline 'The Rise and Rise of the Volag', and the following diagrams show what was sought and what was given or pledged. By great coincidence the same journal published this author's letter in its main issue for 7 July and this was duly noted by

14

...And what they got

Donor Country	New pledges to regular annual assistance programme of UNHCR	Pledges for 3-5 years to development projects in refugee areas
Australia	$2m.	Unspecific.
Austria	$128,000.	$4.9m health infra-structure in Ethiopia.
Belgium	7,000 tonnes of wheat and 5 staff.	
Britain		$6.5m.
Canada	$1.2m.	$10.54m for Zambia, Tanzania, Ethiopia, Botswana, Sudan and Zaire.
China	$1m could go to either.	
Denmark	$1.2m.	$3m.
EEC		Promised nothing but in fact already helping with 1 project worth $3m.
Finland		$10m.
France		$890,000 but indicated further interest in projects worth $15m.
Germany	$2m.	Indicated interest in 6 projects worth $33m.
Holland	$2m.	Unspecific.
Italy		$15m which prompted a French newspaper to say that unlike their own country's more modest pledge, the Italians could not be trusted to deliver.
Japan	$6m.	
Norway	$1.8m.	$3m.
Saudi Arabia	$5m could go to either.	
Sweden	$1.8m.	$3m.
Switzerland		Privately indicated interest in projects worth $7m.
Turkey		$50,000 but indicated interest in a project worth $300,000.
United States		Nothing specific; but private bilateral pledges probably amounted to $40m.
Vatican		$300,000.
Yugoslavia	$310,000 in goods rather than cash.	

both the Sudanese and Somali delegations and permanent representatives.

We come now to what can only be described as an international scandal, namely the forced repatriation of refugees from Djibouti to Ethiopia in which UNHCR is a willing partner and implementer of policies which run directly counter to the long-proclaimed principles of refugee relief and of every humanitarian tenet. *Refouler* is the French word meaning forced return, so that the principle of *non-refoulement* is, and must be, a fundamental norm in safeguarding the freedom and lives of refugees. And yet with regard to Djibouti, this principle is flouted covertly yet trumpeted overtly. At base the situation arose whereby Djibouti, a tiny country dependent upon Ethiopia for trade along the railway to Addis Ababa, felt it could no longer host over 30,000 refugees some of whom had originally fled the so-called 'Ogaden War' of 1977/78, but most of whom flee from the massive oppression and press-ganging which goes on inside Ethiopia. Reference had earlier been made to evidence produced at ICARA II. I witnessed the immediate ejection of the Oromo who was trying so tragically to spread the news, and it is ironic that later in the day the Somali permanent mission and delegation to ICARA II walked out and issued the press release which appears as Appendix 4. Appendix 2 to the official Somali document also has something to say on this subject and it is added as Appendix 5. It could, perhaps, be said that these sources are not entirely disinterested, but Sudan is thousands of miles away from Djibouti across the other side of Ethiopia. Hence further corroboration from that country must be impartial. The July issue of SUDANOW, the official journal of the Sudan Government, published a piece in its July issue. Finally, in August 1984 an Oromo refugee just returned from the region appeared in London and gave a briefing, the content of which forms Appendix 6.

It is an impossibility that all these separate and disparate people and organisations could have met and conspired together to produce this grisly tale, and the total of the evidence is such as to command credulity even from those unwilling to give it.

Next, we must ask ourselves why the Tripartite Commission (Ethiopia, Djibouti and UNHCR) should wish to construct this inhuman exercise; especially Ethiopia which pleads for aid for thousands of refugees, returnees and famine victims. The answer lies in three parts: Ethiopia needs, as said before, to create a humanitarian image and therefore, in this instance, be seen to be welcoming home those of its citizens who previously fled. In reality this is to attract aid; to enable the 'politicals' to be shot or to be impressed into the huge Ethiopian militia and thus forced to fight against their kith and kin. As to Djibouti; this minute country is, as also said before, dependent upon Ethiopia economically and also morally. Djibouti knows full well what Ethiopia could and would do if displeased, and thus has to fall into line while at the same time getting rid of thousands of people who are just not wanted, refugees or otherwise. UNHCR's role is the most despicable, and can only be an attempt to bolster its failing popularity as illustrated by ICARA II. There can be but one recommendation: that this terrible situation be thoroughly investigated by an entirely independent international commission. If the Tripartite Commission has nothing to hide, it will, one presumes, raise no objection. What is certain is that here we have an extremely serious infringement of basic human rights involving the lives, freedom and well-being of more than 30,000 people, many of whom have already been killed, committed suicide or been press-ganged into the Ethiopian militia. If nothing is done any refugee, anywhere, may wonder if he can count upon UNHCR to protect him within its own terms of reference.

Thus, and with sinking heart, we contemplate at least three aspects within which the United Nations has evaded its duty: the deliberate mutilation of an official report; the failure to address root causes of refugee flows at an international conference and, finally, participation in an exercise dubious at best, but inhuman at worst. If this were all, it would be bad enough, but Chapter 5 should reveal a larger and more encompassing evasion which strikes at the very charter of the world body.

Chapter 4

THE EEC AND THE EUROPEAN PARLIAMENT

In contrast to the cosmetic and evasive attitude of the United Nations, the European Community as represented at the European Parliament has done better after a struggle. That struggle began in 1983 when strong rumours circulated as to mis-use of food-aid by Ethiopia which resulted in a demand by the parliament for an investigation. This request was at first refused by Commissioner Edgard Edouard Pisani, the European Commissioner responsible, but when the parliament threatened to suspend the whole Commission (there are fourteen Commissioners) he had no option but to agree. Accordingly a commission led by Monsieur Michel Poniatowski, Chairman of the Committee on Development and Cooperation left for Addis Ababa, and returned with a verdict that nothing was amiss. The commission should have taken more care as there had been other reports of malpractice as regards food-aid from the United Nations agency World Food Programme (WFP). Late in 1983 the Ethiopian Regional Representative for Wollega of the Relief and Rehabilitation Commission defected, and he took with him to Sudan a copy of the instructions he had received about the exact methods to be employed to falsify the accounts. This incriminating document received a small notice in the British *Times*, and although briefly remarked upon, seems to have made little impression. In so far as it must constitute an important insight into Ethiopian methods it is included as Appendix 7.

Meantime, the European parliament was taking more and more interest in The Horn of Africa, as shown by a Resolution on human rights in Ethiopia adopted on 10 May 1979. As further other information flowed in, other Resolutions were adopted. At the same time my private reports on fact-finding missions to Sudan, Egypt and Somalia had been noted as was the mooted formation of a Horn of Africa and Aden Committee. In these circumstances I duly received one of the first drafts of a report being prepared by Sig. Carlo Ripa di Meana MEP a citizen of Venice and a member of the Italian Socialist Party.

Italy has always shown a great interest in Eritrea, as its former colony, and there have been several efforts to try to correct the forcible take-over of Eritrea in defiance of the relevant United Nations resolution. It was not therefore altogether surprising to find that the draft report was narrow through being largely composed of Italian contributions which led it to concentrate almost entirely upon Eritrea with only vague references to the rest of the Horn. I was asked to submit amendments and additions, and these were made on the basis of enlarging the scope of the report to include all that is meant by 'The Horn of Africa' as well as to include some reference at least to the Arabian peninsula which would be at risk if the Horn were ever monopolised by a certain superpower. All of those recommendations were accepted, and were indeed reinforced by events in 1984 and by copies of a further report made by me after another mission to Sudan in February/March 1984.

Meantime, Ethiopia began to exert tremendous pressure to stop the report and the resolution to which it would eventually lead, and messages were sent to both the Italian Government and to the political party to which Sig. Carlo Ripa di Meana belonged. Not content with that, Mr Goshu Wolde, the Ethiopian Foreign Minister, wrote to the President of the European Parliament and to Sig. Rumor, the Chairman of the Political Affairs Committee (upon which Sig. Ripa di Meana sat). I was asked to go again to Strasbourg in April 1984 when the report was to be debated and in the two days immediately previous I saw not one but two Ethiopian ambassadors (from Brussels and Paris) scurrying about trying to lobby anyone whom they thought could be persuaded to interfere with the debate. All these efforts were to no avail and Sig. Ripa di Meana pursued his objective to a victory when, on 12 April 1984, his report led to the adoption of a resolution, the final text of which is shown as Appendix 8. Perusal of the many items will reveal a determination to come to grips with the situation which is greatly to be commended.

However, the June 1984 European elections have changed the face of the European parliament, and every effort must be made so that this resolution is not lost in the files. This is especially important in view of the vituperative note issued by the Ethiopian Government, if only to illustrate the imperative tone adopted by Ethiopia albeit a recipient of European aid.

19

Chapter 5

SELF-DETERMINATION FOR SOMALIS –
AN EVADED DUTY

In the previous chapters, and the appendices to which they refer, an attempt has been made briefly to portray something of Somalia, Ethiopia, the United Nations and the European Community as a backdrop to the main argument which is the core of this work, namely the denial of the right to self-determination for the Somalis in Western Somalia (or Eastern Ethiopia, as the reader may prefer). For the sake of clarity this chapter is divided into a number of sections.

1. Identity of Western Somalia

We are concerned with the legal status of Western Somalia, and the area of issue consists of those regions inhabited by Somalis situated westward and northward of the administrative line drawn in 1950 which were, in principle administered by Ethiopia until the 1977/78 'Ogaden War', and which are now so administered. Later on it will be necessary to examine the status of this area as a 'unit of self-determination', but at this point it is necessary to discuss a factor of considerable importance both legally and politically. This factor may be called the 'limit of claim' while it is understood that Somalia makes no territorial claim upon Ethiopia, but is only invoking the principle of self-determination and thus challenges the validity of the Ethiopian title to the region. This must bring up the point of a precise limit as setting the bounds of Ethiopia and Western Somalia. It does not seem that either the Somali Government nor the Western Somali Liberation Front (WSLF) has made any reference to a geographical limit in any published statement. It has previously been noted that the poetic saying is that 'Western Somalia stops where the camel stops' but, as also argued, this is hardly sufficient for any kind of legal argument. A statement of 'limit of claim' would contribute to the validity of the argument, and it would preclude such a question as 'Where are they going to stop?'. Additionally, such a definite limit would help the argument by indicating the exact end of the Somali 'identity' and thus high-light the social facts behind the argument. Another point which should be clarified is whether or not Harar was populated by Gallas rather than by Somalis. This is mentioned not in so far that Harar is Ethiopian, but in order that people hostile to the argument for self-determination may be precluded from trying to find 'holes' in the overall claim.

Finally, there may be a necessity specifically to prove that the northern limit of the Somali nation is actually at the Awash River and not short of it (i.e. the limit of the Esa tribe).

2. Status of the Somalis in the 19th century

In many cases of decolonisation the process is based upon the idea of reverting to a previous state of affairs, hence it is pertinent to consider the situation in The Horn prior to colonisation, and this also bears on the idea of the Somali as a group with a capacity for self-determination such as would include the Western Somalis, and this turns upon the legal point of whether a territory is subject to the sovereignty of any State, or whether it is an area not yet acquired by any State – the latter being known as *terra nullius*. For instance large areas of Africa were parcelled out between the European Powers during the colonisation period, and they included areas which were *terrae nullius*. Morocco and Ethiopia have been accepted as the exceptions which prove the rule. In the 19th century it was European practice to accept the legal personality of a variety of African political entities such as the Swazi Kingdom, the Basutos, Lobengula's kingdom, Khama's Country, the kingdoms of Rwanda and Burundi, Uganda, Dahomey and Ashanti, and resort was usually made to treaty-making as a preliminary to political take-overs. It should be noted that the very incidence of making treaties meant the recognition of existing entites in Africa. However, not all traditional African social forms were States in International law, and the Somalis did not exhibit the signs of statehood prior to colonial expansion in East Africa for the reason that while the Somalis showed strong elements of solidarity, there was no hierarchical government. For this reason the Somali evident nationhood was not accompanied by statehood. But irrespective of that, the Somali country was not a *terra nullius* in international law. This is a most important point which assists two other questions:

(a) the area south of the Awash river was not under Ethiopian sovereignty,

(b) the region of the Somali tribes was not available for acquisition as

21

being a *terra nullius*, i.e. open territory to be freely taken over by anyone.

From this it can be seen that as there were no treaties of cession, Ethiopian expansion would disturb the *status quo* and therefore constitute conquest of existing legal entities.

There is some recent authoritative evidence supporting the legal position outlined in the previous paragraph. In the Advisory Opinion of the International Court of Justice concerning *Western Sahara*, October 16, 1975, I.C.J. Reports, 1975, p.12, the Court was called upon to examine whether, in the period beginning in 1884, Western Sahara was 'a territory belonging to no one (*terra nullius*)'.

The answer given by the Court is of great significance since the situation in the region was very similar to that of the Somali Country in the same period. Consequently the key passages must be given in full (Advisory Opinion, pp. 38-39, paragraphs 79-81:

'79. Turning to Question 1, the Court observes that the request specifically locates the question in the context of 'the time of colonization by Spain', and it therefore seems clear that the words 'Was Western Sahara . . . a territory belonging to no one (*terra nullius*)?' have to be interpreted by reference to the law in force at that period. The expression '*terra nullius*' was a legal term of art employed in connection with 'occupation' as one of the accepted legal methods of acquiring sovereignty over territory. 'Occupation' being legally an original means of peaceably acquiring sovereignty over territory otherwise than by cession or succession, it was a cardinal condition of a valid 'occupation' that the territory should be *terra nullius* – a territory belonging to no-one – at the time of the act alleged to constitute the 'occupation' (cf. *Legal Status of Eastern Greenland*, P.C.I.J., Series A/B, No. 53, pp. 44f. and 63f.). In the view of the Court, therefore, a determination that Western Sahara was a '*terra nullius*' at the time of colonization by Spain would be possible only if it were established that at that time the territory belonged to no-one in the sense that it was then open to acquisition through the legal process of 'occupation'.

'80. Whatever differences of opinion there may have been amongst jurists, the State practice of the relevant period indicates that territories inhabited by tribes or people having a social and political organisation were not regarded as *terrae nullius*. It shows that in the case of such territories the acquisition of sovereignty was not generally considered as effected unilaterally through 'occupation' of *terra nullius* by original title but through agreements concluded with local rulers. On occasion, it is true, the word 'occupation' was used in a non-technical sense denoting simply acquisition of sovereignty; but that did not signify that the acquisition of sovereignty through such agreements with authorities of the country was regarded as an 'occupation' of a '*terra nullius*' in the proper sense of these terms. On the contrary, such agreements with local rulers, whether or not considered as an actual 'cession' of the territory, were regarded as derivative roots of title, and not original titles obtained by occupation of *terrae nullius*.

'81. In the present instance, the information furnished to the Court shows that at the time of colonization Western Sahara was inhabited by peoples which, if nomadic, were socially and politically organized in tribes and under chiefs competent to represent them. It also shows that, in colonising Western Sahara, Spain did not proceed on the basis that it was establishing its sovereignty over *terrae nullius*. In its Royal Order of 26 December 1884, far from treating the case as one of occupation of *terra nullius*, Spain proclaimed that the King was taking the Rio de Oro under his protection on the basis of agreements which had been entered into with the chiefs of the local tribes: the Order referred expressly to 'the documents which the independent tribes of this part of the coast' had 'signed with the representative of the Sociedad Española de Africanistas', and announced that the King had confirmed 'the deeds of adherence' to Spain. Likewise, in negotiating with France concerning the limits of Spanish territory to the north of the Rio de Oro, that is, in the Sakiet El Hamra area, Spain did not rely upon any claim to the acquisition of sovereignty over a *terra nullius*.'

In these passages the Court adopts the view that 'territory inhabited by tribes or peoples having a social and political organisation were not regarded as *terrae nullius*'. Put in another form the proposition is that legal status of some kind may exist in the absence of statehood. Moreover the Court was referring explicitly to the position in international law obtaining in the late nineteenth century.

A further issue placed before the International Court in the *Western Sahara* proceedings concerned the existence of 'legal ties' which existed between Western Sahara, at the time of its colonisation by Spain, and the 'Mauritanian entity'. In the proceedings Mauritania expressly accepted that the 'Mauritanian entity' did not then constitute a State and also that eventual independence of Mauritania 'was not retroactive'. As a consequence the International Court was bound to consider 'the legal nature of the "Mauritanian entity" . . . ' (Advisory Opinion, I.C.J. Reports, 1975, pp. 57-65, paragraphs 130-152). Given the similarity between the peoples of the region of Mauritania and those of the Somali Country, in both cases nomadic tribes with well-defined migration areas, the pronouncements of the International Court have direct relevance to the status of the Somalis in the pre-colonial period.

The Mauritanian Government, in the course of the *Western Sahara* proceedings, identified the 'Mauritanian entity' as the Shinguitti Country, 'which constituted a distinct human unit, characterised by a common language, way of life and religion' and also 'a uniform social structure' (I.C.J. Reports, 1975, p.58). Whilst the tribes concerned were not held out as constituting a State, Mauritania maintained that the tribes and emirates were independent and did not have ties of allegiance to the Sultan of Morocco. The Shinguitti Country, according to Mauritania was:

'[A] community having its own cohesion, its own special characteristics, and a common Saharan law concerning the use of water-holes, grazing lands and agricultural lands, the regulation of inter-tribal hostilities and the settlement of disputes.'

(I.C.J. Reports, 1975, p.59)

In further expounding the views advanced by Mauritania in the *Western Sahara* case, the International Court reports.

'If it is thought necessary to have recourse to verbal classifications, Mauritania suggests that the concepts of "nation" and "people" would be the most appropriate to explain the position of the Shinguitti people at the time of colonization; they would most nearly describe an entity which despite its political diversity bore the characteristics of an independent nation, a people formed of tribes, confederations and emirates jointly exercising co-sovereignty over the Shinguitti country.'

(I.C.J. Reports, 1975, p.60, paragraph 138)

The conclusions of the Court on the status of the 'Mauritanian entity' were as follows:

'148. In the case concerning *Reparation for Injuries Suffered in the Service of the United Nations*, the Court observed: "the subjects of law in any legal system are not necessarily identical in their nature or in the extent of their rights, and their nature depends upon the needs of the community." (I.C.J. Reports, 1949, p.178). In examining the propositions of Mauritania regarding the legal nature of the Bilad Shinguitti or Mauritanian entity, the Court gives full weight both to that observation and to the special characteristics of the Saharan region and peoples with which the present proceedings are concerned. Some criterion has, however, to be employed to determine in any particular case whether what confronts the law is or is not legally an "entity". The Court, moreover, notes that in the *Reparation* case the criterion which it applied was to enquire whether the United Nations Organization – the entity involved – was in "such a position that it possesses, in regard to its Members, rights which it is entitled to ask them to respect" (*ibid.*). In that Opinion, no doubt, the criterion was applied in somewhat special context. Nevertheless, it expresses the essential test where a group, whether composed of States, of tribes or of individuals, is claimed to be a legal entity distinct from its members.

'149. In the present case, the information before the Court discloses that, at the time of the Spanish colonisation, there existed many ties of a racial, linguistic, religious, cultural and economic nature between various tribes and emirates whose peoples dwelt in the Saharan region which today is comprised within the Territory of Western Sahara and the Islamic Republic of Mauritania. It also discloses, however, the independence of the emirates and many of the tribes in relation to one another and, despite some forms of common activity, the absence among them of any common institutions or organs, even of a quite minimal character. Accordingly, the Court is unable to find that the information before it provides any basis for considering the emirates and tribes which existed in the region to have constituted, in another phrase used by the Court in the *Reparation* case, "an entity capable of availing itself of obligations incumbent upon its Members" (*ibid.*). Whether the Mauritanian entity is described as the Bilad Shinguitti, or as the Shinguitti "nation", as Mauritania suggests, or as some form of league or association, the difficulty remains that it did not have the character of a personality or corporate entity distinct from the several emirates and tribes which composed it. The proposition, therefore, that the Bilad Shinguitti should be considered as having been a Mauritanian "entity" enjoying some form of sovereignty in Western Sahara is not one that can be sustained.'

(I.C.J. Reports, 1975, p. 63)

This rather negative conclusion requires evaluation, as it would have been advantageous to Somalia if the Shinguitti Country (or 'Mauritanian entity') had been seen as a 'legal entity distinct from its members'. It is possible to argue that the Somali tribes are more homogenous than the units composing the Shinguitti element: which is to say to find a distinction in the Western Sahara findings on the facts. But on evidence available in written works it is not easy to argue that the Somalis as a whole constituted an entity with 'common institutions or organs', 'capable of availing itself of obligations incumbent upon its members', 'a corporate entity distinct from the several . . . tribes which composed it'. One is therefore inclined to see in the 'segmentary lineage system', which was nation-wide, and the existence of a treaty, the organs of a minimal character such as are required by the International Court in its Advisory Opinion in the Western Sahara case. Whatever the ins and outs of this may be, the thinking of the Court concerning the legal personality of the 'Mauritanian entity' does not detract from its previous statement that 'Territories inhabited by tribes or peoples having a special or political organisation were not regarded as *terra nullius*. The foregoing remarks were intended to give some kind of Advisory Opinion in the Western Sahara case, and there can be no doubt that a kind of advocacy could be based on the assertion that the Somali nation, in the pre-colonial period, would have satisfied the requirements for legal personality prescribed by the International Court. As regards the Western Sahara case, it can be taken that Mauritania was in that case trying to establish a legal personality of 'confederacy', which is a grouping of units, but failed in that effort. Therefore the findings of the Court are not inimical to the opinion that individual Somali tribes were legal entities which, even as separate units, had 'common institutions or organs'.

3. Status of the Somalis – Political frontiers of Ethiopia

What must be essential to this argument is an investigation of the legal effects of colonial advancement upon the Horn of Africa, and the Somali country in particular, which special reference to the boundaries of Ethiopia and the Somali country before 1884, for that was the year when British and Italian influence began to appear whereas it was after 1886 that the process of Ethiopian expansion started. It is correct to refer to 'territorial boundaries' as Ethiopia was seen as having statehood while although not having statehood, the Somali tribal areas were not *terrae nullius*. What it is important to note is that the Ethiopian frontier was the river Awash before the conquests of Menelik II. Next it is a requirement to examine evidence concerning the southern frontier of Ethiopia:

(a) Contemporary witnesses

Probably the best such witnesses was Sir Richard Burton in his book *First Footsteps in East Africa* published in 1856, which contains a treasury of detailed observation of the region and its people. It is a common opinion that Burton was the leading Arabist of his day. In that book Burton gives an account of his journey from Aden to Harar in 1854-55, and he makes no mention of any Ethiopian presence in northern Somalia, nor does he note any links between the Somali tribes and the Ethiopians, neither is there any reference to Ethiopians either as minority residents nor even as traders. Had they been present one may be sure that Burton would have noted them.

(b) Contemporary geographers

In the Foreign Office Confidential Print there is an item dated December 3, 1890, and entitled 'Memorandum respecting the Southern Boundaries of Abyssinia' (See Appendix 9). This contains a collection of excerpts from works of reference published in the years preceding the compilation. None of these items refers to the dominion of Shoa (the Southern Ethiopian Kingdom) over Somali areas, although a number describe Shoan encroachments, in episodes, upon various sections of the Galla tribes. In a work published in 1887, and quoted in the Memorandum, Professor Fasolo describes the region of Abyssinia:

Abyssinia and the Italian Colonies on the Red Sea, Caserta. No reference is made to Somali areas. In the map attached to the work Shoa is shown bounded on the south by the River Hawash (or Awash). The Galla tribes to the south of the Ethiopian dominians 'are not marked as being tributary to any State' in the words of the Memorandum.

(c) Contemporary maps

Maps which have a reputable source and of a high technical standard constitute 'expert opinion' in legal terms in which cartography is of the essence of any report, and they provide direct evidence of the condition of knowledge or belief as to political facts at any given period. This, of course, is of particular importance in cases of territorial dispute when, naturally, such evidence must be taken with other evidence. Two cases where maps played a significant part in modern law concerning boundaries include the 'Rann of Kutch Arbitration (1968) and the Beagle Channel Arbitration (1977) in which last case both the Governments of Chile and Argentina produced a wealth of cartographical evidence. In both these cases the evidence of maps related particularly to the latter half of the 19th century when the production of maps was of a high standard. In the decade or so before the colonial penetration of the Somali country, which started in 1884, a number of maps showed the southern boundary of Ethiopia as the river Awash. The following are thought to be a sample of authoritative cartography of that period:

    (i) *The 'Dispatch' Atlas.* Vol. II, 'Africa' sheet, no date. Presented to the Royal Geographical Society, London, 1858.

    (ii) *Egypt and Equatorial Africa.* Compiled from 'original surveys and the best authenticated sources' by John Fowler, 1877, Covent Garden.

    (iii) *The Royal Atlas of Modern Geography.* By Alexander Keith Johnson. Edinburgh and London. 1879.
Sheet 42: 'Upper Nubia and Abyssinia'
See also *Sheet 39*: 'Africa'.

    (iv) *Stieler's Handatlas.* Gotha. Justus Perthes. This publication has particular authority, and emanates from a well known cartographical publishing house.
6th edition, 1875. Plate No. 70, 'Nordost-Afrika und Arabien'. This Plate is reproduced in Annex II. Abyssinia and Shoa are distinctly shown and are carefully distinguished from the regions designated as 'Galla-Länder' and 'Somali-Länder'. See also Plate No. 68 relating to Africa as a whole.
7th edition, 1882. This also contains Plates No. 68 and 70 in the same form.

Note: the relevant plates in the editions of 1891 and 1894 show a relatively small expansion of Ethiopian territory.

(v) *A Map of Eastern Equatorial Africa*. Compiled by E.G. Ravenstein. Published for the Royal Geographical Society by Edward Stanford, London. 1882. The individual sheets are dated. A proportion of the sheets show tribal areas with no indication of Ethiopian presence: see sheets East 4, 5, 6, 10, 11 and 14.

(vi) *Andrees Handatlas*. 1881.

See the Plates at pp. 93, 94-95, and also the Supplementary Plate at pp. 28-29.

(vii) *W.G. Blackie: The Comprehensive Atlas and Geography of the World*. London. 1882.

Plate 45: 'The Nile Valley . . . including the Chief Part of Nubia with Abyssinia'. This shows Abyssinia (including Shoa) with a distinct limit well to the west of Harar, with a modest salient southward to the latitude 8° North, into the Galla country.

(viii) *A Map of the Nile from the Equatorial Lakes to the Mediterranean*. Edward Stanford. 1883. Ethiopia is shown with a southern boundary on the River Hawash.

(ix) *Nouvelle Carte de l'Egypte et de ses Dépendances*, 1:3,000,000. 3 sheets. Berlin. S. Schropp (J.H. Neumann). 1885.

Feuille 2. Soudan égyptien et Abyssinie.

(x) *Egypt and the Basin of the Nile*.

Constructed by W. and A.K. Johnston. Edinburgh and London. No date. However, the map was received by the Royal Geographical Society in 1885: see the *Proceedings of the R.G.S.*, Vol. VII, No. 4, April 1885. The scale is 52 miles to the inch. The map is on linen and is well produced, by a leading map publishing house. The political situation is indicated very clearly by colouring. Abyssinia is bounded by the River Hawash. To the south and east, marked in prominent lettering is 'Somali Land' an attribution extending over the entire Horn of Africa *and* including Harar.

(xi) *Atlas von Afrika*. A. Hartleben's Verlag. 1886. Sheet XII. 'Die Länder am Obern Nil und Abessinien'.

(xii) *Schoa und die dem Konig Menelek Tributarem Gebeite*. 1876-81. Justus Perthes, Habenicht, M. Petermann. 1886. This is an important item and is thus reproduced in the Foreign Office 'Memorandum respecting the Southern Boundaries of Abyssinia' of 1890 (see, again, Appendix 9).

(d) Modern anthropological experts

The expert opinion of modern anthropologists is that the Somali country, before the colonial era, was not under Ethiopian control or suzerainty in any form, and as to that attention is invited to Professor I.M.
Lewis's *A Pastoral Democracy* published in 1961, pp. 15-19.

(e) Evidence of professional historians

In Section 4 reference will be made to incontrovertible evidence that in
the years 1886-92 the Emperor Menelik launched a deliberate, sustained and successful campaign of conquest against Harar and the Somali country. All historical accounts are clear and unanimous in the fact
that previous to Menelik's conquests, the Somali tribes were totally free
from Ethiopian and Shoan control.

(f) Typonomy of Western Somalia

The origin of place names sometimes bears out other evidence in territorial disputes. It is here most significant to note that the Ogaden is
named after a Darod clan of that name. What is even more significant is
the entire absence of any Ethiopian place names in the Somali country.

(g) The opinion of Emperor Haile Selassie I of Ethiopia

In the 1976 Oxford University Press edition of The Autobiography of
Emperor Haile Selassie I, page 14 shows Haile Selassie's description of
his father's operations in the Harar region in the Ogaden, and the
Emperor stated:
'(Menelik) then secured the Ogaden which had not yet been incorpo-
rated within Harar province.'

All the above show that Western Somalia was never under Ethiopian
rule.

4. Colonial advances by Ethiopia, Britain, Italy and France 1884-1892

The purpose of this section is to sketch the general pattern of foreign
intervention in the Horn of Africa and then to place the Ethiopian Conquests of 1886-1892 in a proper historical, political and legal context.
The Menelik expansion may then be appreciated for what it was: an
integral part of the diplomacy of partition of the Somali country. In

what follows the short period of Egyptian control of the northern coast of the Somali country in the years 1874-1884 is ignored as being of no significance.

(a) British encroachment

The process of penetration by Great Britain may be summarised as follows:

(i) The conclusion of Treaties of Protection with the Somali Tribes between 1884 and 1886. The precise significance of these treaties will be considered in Section 5 of this work. In general political terms they conferred a right of pre-emption upon the British Government, that is to say, the Somali tribes undertook to cede territory to the British Government and no other.

(ii) The Notification to the Powers that a British Protectorate had been established from 'Ras Jiburti . . . to Bunder Ziadeh, in the 49th meridian of east longitude (Greenwich)'; dated July 20, 1887.

(iii) An Anglo-French Exchange of Notes on February 2 and 9, 1888, defining their respective spheres of influence on the Somali coast.

(iv) The Anglo-Italian Protocol of April 15, 1891, defining the respective spheres of influence in Eastern Africa.

The text is in Hertslet, *Map of Africa by Treaty*, III, p. 949.

This arrangement envisaged the partition and eventual extinction of Ethiopia as a State.

(v) The Anglo-Italian Protocol of May 5, 1894, defining their respective spheres of influence in Eastern Africa.

The text is in Hertslet, III, p. 951.

This instrument defines the boundary between the British sphere of influence on the Gulf of Aden, subsequently to become the Protectorate of British Somaliland, and the Italian sphere in the east and on the south (the Ogaden).

(vi) The Anglo-Ethiopian Treaty of May 14, 1897, and Exchange of Notes of June 4, 1897.

The texts of these agreements are to be found in Hertslet, I, pp. 423-29.

In substance this substituted Ethiopia for Italy as the southern neighbour of British Somaliland. The arrangements were a consequence of Menelik's victory over the Italians at Adowa and the unwillingness of the British Government to make any effective challenge to Menelik's territorial claims in the regions of Harar and the Ogaden.

(b) Italian encroachment

The development of Italian interest related both to Eritrea (Danakil Coast) and to the Somali Country. In the account which follows the Eritrean episode is ignored. However, it is relevant in a general way in providing further evidence of European intervention. The process of penetration by Italy in the Somali and Galla regions may be summarised as follows:

(i) Treaties of Protection with various local rulers, including certain Somali tribes, 1884-95.

See the list in Hertslet, III, pp. 1086-87.

(ii) Italy gains control of certain Concessions granted and powers vested in the Sultan of Zanzibar in respect of the Benadir Ports, 1890-96.

(iii) The Anglo-Italian Protocol of April 15, 1891, defining their respective spheres of influence in Eastern Africa:

(iv) The Anglo-Italian Protocol of May 5, 1894, defining their respective spheres of influence in Eastern Africa:

(v) The Italo-Ethiopian Treaty of Peace signed on October 26, 1896.

The text is in Hertslet, I, p. 458.

This instrument was the consequence of Italian defeat at Adowa. By Article III Italy recognised Ethiopia as a sovereign and independent State. The question of delimitation of frontiers was reserved for subsequent agreement. The subsequent agreement was to take the form of the Treaty signed on May 16, 1908:

(c) French encroachment

The French colonial possession known as French Somaliland, or Djibouti, or the Territory of the Afars and Issas, evolved as follows:

(i) Treaty of Cession, France and the Danakil Chiefs, relating to Obock, March 11, 1862.

(ii) French Notice of the Limits of French Possessions at Obock, December 2, 1880.

(iii) Treaties of Protection concluded with Sultans of Gobad and Tajurah, 1884-85, and cessions to France by these Rulers: see Hertslet, *Map of Africa by Treaty*, II, pp. 630-33.

(iv) Treaty of Friendship and Protection between France and the Chiefs of the Issa Somalis, March 26, 1885: see Hertslet, II, p. 633.

(v) Frontier Agreement, France and Ethiopia, March 20, 1897.

For the text see Hertslet II, p. 421. This agreement established the frontier between the French Protectorate and Ethiopia, from the Red Sea (the frontier with Eritrea not being settled at that time) and the tripoint with the Protectorate of British Somaliland.

(d) Ethiopian encroachment

The preceding accounts, in outline, of European intervention in East Africa provide a necessary framework for an understanding of the policy of Menelik II, the Emperor of Ethiopia. The chronology, in particular, is important. Menelik's policy involved two simple objectives: resistance to European territorial pressures, that is survival as a sovereign, and an expansion, probably pre-emptive in character in relation to the European Powers, but substantially based upon Menelik's own programme of territorial expansion.

Both by force of circumstances and by inclination Menelik participated, with much skill and marked success, in the colonial partition of the Danakil region, the Somali Country, and the Galla areas to the south of Shoa.

The evidence must now be considered, reliance being placed upon secondary sources in the form of professional historians. Of the general aims of Menelik, Professor Edward Ullendorff has this to say (*The Ethiopians*, 3rd ed. 1973. pp. 89-90):

The general aims of Menelik's enlightened policy were threefold: (1) to contain the European powers on the borders of his country and to safeguard Ethiopia's independence . . . ; (2) *the permanent conquest, followed by the establishment of effective Ethiopian authority*, [emphasis supplied], of the neighbouring Muslim and pagan areas in the south; and (3) internal administrative reforms . . .

Already during King John's reign Menelik had started on the systematic conquest of the fertile regions to the west and south of Shoa. This policy was continued during the first years of his own reign, when the rich territory in the southern Awash Valley and the Sidama and Janjero areas were annexed. In 1897 followed the conquest of the Kingdom of Kaffa which had held out for so long . . .

After the defeat of the Italians at Adowa, Salisbury reacted by ordering the reconquest of the Sudan. At this period when British policy was centred upon control of the Nile Valley, Menelik was regarded by British policy makers in exactly the same way as Italy: as a power to be reckoned with and kept neutral, at least, in relation to conflicts in which Britain was involved. Thus the question arose, would Italy appear as an ally of France in the competition for control of the Sudan? Likewise, the question was raised by Salisbury in 1897, was it possible to keep Menelik neutral in the struggle with the Mahdi? This was in fact the object of Rodd's mission to Menelik: see Appendix 10.

Generally the diplomatic relations of Menelik at this period are explained with great clarity and an abundance of documentation by Robinson, Gallagher and Denny, *Africa and the Victorians: The Official Mind of Imperialism*, 1961, pp. 325, 331, 344, 346-50, 359-61, 364-65, 368-69. After Adowa Menelik was taken into account in the standard diplomatic calculations of the time. Ethiopia, like other Powers at this period, could be placated, as was the custom, by territorial concessions. In the treaties of 1896 and 1897 not only did Menelik's southern conquests receive effective recognition but France, Great Britain and Italy were forced to make *concessions* in terms of *the* pre-Adowa status quo: see, for example App 10 Rodd to Salisbury, Despatch 35, June 4, 1897.

A further substantial account of Menelik's place in diplomacy may be found in the work edited by Gann and Duignan, *Colonialism in Africa 1870-1960*, Vol. I, Cambridge, 1969, pp. 420-55, a chapter written by Harold G. Marcus. Of particular interest is the section (pp. 447-53) entitled 'The building of a new Ethiopian Empire'. Mr Marcus states, at page 448, that 'after Aduwa, Menilek's policy was to construct a protective buffer zone around the highlands'.

Mr Marcus in the work referred to and also in his monograph, *The Life and Times of Menelik II*, Oxford, 1975, describes the *process* of Ethiopian conquest in great detail. Two points stand out. The first is the dating of the conquest of Harar and the Ogaden region. Harar was captured in January 1887 (see Marcus, last cited work, pp. 89-93). The conquest of the Haud was completed in 1892 (see Marcus, pp. 136-9). In his works Marcus gives details also of the style of Ethiopian administration of subject peoples and there are clear parallels with the behaviour of colonial administrations in other parts of Africa.

5. Legal personality of Somali tribes during colonialism

The status of the Somali people in the pre-colonial era can be summarised as follows:
   (a) The Somali Country was not under Ethiopian sovereignty;
   (b) The region was not *terra nullius* but was occupied by organized communities;
   (c) The Somali people as a whole did not have statehood and, again as a grouping, probably lacked legal personality in any other form.

However, as has been previously said, the conclusions summarised above were not incompatible with the view that the individual Somali tribes were legal entities which, as separate units, had 'common institutions or organs'. It is now appropriate to examine to what extent the encroaching colonial powers in their practice acknowledged the legal personality of individual Somali tribes.

At least in the early stages of penetration the evidence strongly suggests that such acknowledgement occurred, primarily in the conclusion of 'treaties of protection' which presumed the legal personality, on the plane of international relations, of both contracting parties. That this should be so is by no means surprising or exceptional in view of British dealings with traditional polities in Africa such as the Swazi, the Zulu, the Basutos, Khama and Lobengula.

The British Government concluded a good number of treaties with the tribes in northern Somali Country: standard texts are set forth in Appendix 11 based upon material in the *British and Foreign State Papers*. There is a list of Treaties in Hertslet, *Map of Africa by Treaty*, 3rd ed., I, p. 409. Sir Edward Hertslet, then Foreign Office Librarian, refers to the agreements as Treaties and as such most of them were published in the official series, the *British and Foreign State Papers*. The logical presumption can only be that at the time of conclusion the Somali Tribe in each case was possessed of a capacity to conclude Treaties valid on the plane of international law. The same analysis applies to the Treaties concluded by the Italian Government with Somali tribes.

It is a fact that the treaties concluded by the British Government with the various Somali tribes do not indicate that a surrender of separate existence was taking place, and no cession of territory is provided for. Indeed the clause according to which dispositions of territorial rights by way of cession or in other ways shall only be possible if the British government as the grantee establishes:

(a) that no cession of the area to Great Britain had occurred as a result of the Treaty of Protection,

(b) that the power of disposition remained, in principle at least, with the tribe concerned.

It could generally be said that the arrangements were similar to treaties of friendship and commerce.

Historians relate that in studying the detailed terms of many such treaties among northern nomadic Somali, there has not been one which discusses transactions in land. It has also been said that Somali clans do not traditionally own grazing land. Land is considered by the Somali as a 'gift of God' for the use and enjoyment of all, a concept which is entirely in accordance with nomadic tradition in the same way as it applies to wells or to pasture. Partly irrelevant although this is, it nevertheless supports the previous paragraph, although not being in any way decisive as treaties may not be governed by the domestic laws of the parties.

34

There is no principle of international law which is inimical to the analysis presented in the paragraph above. The better statements of international law avoid generalizations about the effects of treaties of protection. Thus Oppenheim, *International Law*, Vol. I, 1905, p. 138 (para. 93) states the position as follows:-

The position of a State under protectorate within the Family of Nations cannot be defined by a general rule, since it is the treaty of protectorate which indirectly specialises it by enumerating the reciprocal rights and duties of the protecting and the protected State. Each case must therefore be treated according to its own merits.

This statement of principle applies equally to legal personalities other than States. For other statements on similar lines see: Hall, *International Law*, 8th ed., 1924, pp. 150-2; Fawcett, *The British Commonwealth in International Law*, 1963, p. 117.

However, whilst the status of the Somali tribes at the time of the conclusion of the treaties in the period 1884-86 is not to be underestimated, the significance of the Treaties of Protection has to be appreciated in the light of certain other factors. The first is the technical consideration that, although no cession was involved, nor extinction of the personality of the Somali Contracting Party in each case, nonetheless it would still be possible to conclude that the *result* of the agreement was a distribution or fragmentation of the 'Sovereignty' of the given Tribe. The severe restriction on the power of cession is indicative of a distribution of sovereign rights in the significant sphere of 'external' sovereignty. On the concept of divisible sovereignty in relation to protectorates reference may be made to Lord McNair, *International Law Opinions*, 1956, Vol. I, p. 47 (Colonial Office Memorandum dated February 1892) at p. 50 (para 16).

There is yet another factor, which is of critical significance. Assuming that the original Treaties of Protection were genuine and not disguised annexations and that the legal personality of each Somali Contracting Party was not extinguished, these conditions would not prevent the British Government from gaining title by *subsequent* usurpation and consolidation of title, *recognized by other states*, and (perhaps) acquiesced in by some of the Somali Contracting Parties. This is exactly how many colonial titles were obtained. It should be remembered that rights in international law depend upon the principles of that law applicable *at the material time*. The process referred to above was perfectly in tune with the doctrine of contemporary international law. Thus in Oppenheim, *International Law*, 1905, Vol. I, pp. 280-81, it is accepted that protectorates may be precursors of future occupations.

The evidence strongly points to the probability that by 1897 the British protectorate in Somaliland was held in sovereignty in terms of international law. Part of this evidence takes the form of the arrangements concerning frontiers concluded by Ethiopia, Great Britain and Italy in the period following 1896, and these will be referred to again later. The remainder of the evidence consists of a general pattern of conduct on the part of Great Britain and other states which evidently derived from the view that British Somaliland was a colonial protectorate over which Great Britain had sovereignty. The same considerations apply to Italian Somaliland.

In view of the considerations previously advanced, it is not thought that there is any legal significance in the fact that one or more tribes escaped the conclusion of the Treaty of Protection, and this appears to have been the case with the Dulbahante. However, the non-existence of a Treaty of Protection in some cases, taken together with the general evidence of resistance by the Somalis to the imposition of British rule subsequent to the original Treaties of Protection, provides some useful evidence of the Somali national pride and consciousness in connection with the arguments to come which concern self-determination.

6. The Menelik circular letter of 10 April 1891

At this point it is necessary to make an evaluation of a document known as the *Menelik Circular*. The text in an English translation, is to be found in Appendix 10. The document was sent by the Emperor Menelik II to the Heads of State of Great Britain, France, Germany, Italy and Russia. It purported to define the frontiers of Ethiopia. The recipient Governments appear to have ignored the Circular, though the reasons for the silence are unknown.

The evidence is that in origin and purpose the Circular was a statement of a sphere of influence, a programme of *expansion*. In the Somali Government's publication *The Portion of Somali Territory under Ethiopian Colonization* (Mogadishu, June 1974), at pages 12-13, Italian diplomatic archives are quoted which establish that Italy suggested that the Emperor stake out his claims in anticipation of the extension of influence by European powers. This occurred in 1890 at a time when the Italian Government expected that Ethiopia would act as a client and agent for Italian influence. This episode adds to the evidence set forth earlier in this text to the effect that Ethiopia played an integral part in the diplomacy of colonial partition and the assertion of spheres of influence in East Africa.

That Menelik acted upon his Circular in his conquests and in the course of his negotiations with Rodd in 1897 (see Rodd's Despatch No. 15 to Salisbury, in Appendix 10 of this work) is no evidence of the validity of the frontier descriptions contained in it. Indeed, the text of the Circular makes abundantly clear the fact that the Emperor was stating a programme of future expansion, no doubt loosely related to his own conception of the ancient limits of Ethiopia. Thus Menelik stated in the Circular:

While tracing to-day the actual boundaries of my Empire, I shall endeavour, if God gives me life and strength, to re-establish the ancient frontiers (tributaries) of Ethiopia up to Kartoum, and as far as Lake Nyanza with all the Gallas.

Certainly the Circular refers to 'the Arussi country up to the limits of the Somalis, including also the Province of Ogaden'. It will be appreciated that in 1891, when the Circular was disseminated, the Ethiopians were in the process of conquering the Ogaden.

7. The legal character of the boundary arrangements involving Ethiopia, Great Britain and Italy, 1896-1903

In the previous sections certain aspects of the period of colonial encroachment on the Somali Country have been considered, and, in particular, the Ethiopian participation in the diplomacy of penetration and partition has been highlighted. It is now necessary to look more closely at the terminal phase of colonial encroachment and partition. In the period 1896 to 1908 Britain, France and Italy found that frontier delimitations, often involving concessions to Menelik, were the inevitable aftermath of Adowa and the failure of the European powers to subdue and partition Ethiopia. In the Treaties of the period the outcome is the confirmation in principle of the partition of the Horn of Africa between Britain, France, Italy and Ethiopia. For sufficiently obvious reasons only the arrangements involving Britain, Italy and Ethiopia will be examined.

(a) Treaty of Peace, Italy and Ethiopia, 26 October 1896.

The text, in French, is in Hertslet, *Map of Africa by Treaty*, II, p. 458. This instrument ended the state of war between Italy and Ethiopia and Ethiopia was accorded recognition by Italy as a sovereign and independent State. In Article IV the Contracting Parties agreed to postpone the definitive settlement of frontiers and until such settlement the *status quo* was to be maintained. The assumption underlying this provision seems to have been that the two States had a power of disposition over territories under their control: in other words they were possessed of rights of sovereignty over the relevant areas. This view receives strong support from Article V by which Italy agreed, pending the determination of frontiers, not to make cessions to any other Power: in case Italy decided to abandon any territory, this was to be transferred to Ethiopia.

(b) Treaty Between Great Britain and Ethiopia, 14 May, 1897, and Exchange of Notes of 4 June, 1897.

For the English texts see Hertslet, *Map of Africa by Treaty*, I, pp. 423-9. The discussions preceding the conclusion of this agreement are recorded in the despatches of Rodd to be found in App. 10.

Whilst it is a matter of appreciation and there may be some room for doubt, Rodd is seen to be talking about the issue of sovereignty over territory and thus employs the language of *cession, frontiers,* and *territorial claims.* The terms of the Menelik Circular of 1891 are discussed. Clearly at this period the British Protectorate was regarded both by Great Britain and Ethiopia as subject to British sovereignty.

The provisions of the Treaty as concluded reinforce this view of the matter. Article I refers to 'the territories' of the Contracting Parties. Article II refers to 'the frontiers of the British Protectorate on the Somali Coast recognised by the Emperor Menelik'.

One is aware of the fact that in the annexes to this Treaty one British Government extracted a promise from Ethiopia that tribes in any territory transferred would receive 'equitable treatment':

However, it is abundantly clear that the tribes were regarded as the population of territory involved in a change of sovereignty who would become 'subjects of Ethiopia'.

(c) Agreement between Great Britain and Italy respecting the Benadir Coast and Jurisdiction in Zanzibar, 13 January, 1905.

For the English text see Hertslet, *Map of Africa by Treaty*, III, p. 954. This Exchange of Notes constituting an Agreement is expressed to relate to 'the purchase by the Italian Government of all the sovereign and other rights of His Highness the Sultan of Zanzibar over the towns, ports and territory of the Benadir Coast . . . ' Moreover, Great Britain was granted a right of pre-emption in respect of the territory and other items in question. These arrangements provide cogent evidence of the assertion at this period of rights amounting to sovereignty in respect of the territory they controlled by both Great Britain and Italy.

(d) Agreement Between Great Britian, France and Italy, respecting Abyssinia, 13 December, 1906.

For the French text see Hertslet, *op. cit.*, II, p. 436. An English translation appears in *The Somali Peninsula*, 1962, p. 107. In the preamble to this Agreement reference is made to 'the British, French and Italian possessions bordering on Ethiopia'. The general purpose of the Agreement is to confirm the status quo resulting from the various earlier agreements governing territorial dispositions and frontiers in the region of East Africa: see the provisions of Articles I and IV. The Agreement of 1906 represents the final stage in the confirmation and legitimisation of the colonial partition of the Somali Country, a process in which Ethiopia had played an important role. Consequently in the present arrangement Ethiopia, though not a Contracting Party, was accorded an appropriately prominent place. The instrument provides further confirmation of the view on the part of the states concerned that the territories involved were under their full sovereignty.

(e) Convention Between Ethiopia and Italy settling the Frontier Between the Italian Possessions of Somalia and the Ethiopian Empire, 16 May, 1908.

This agreement appears, in an English translation, in *British and Foreign State Papers*, Vol. 101, p. 1000. The preamble contains the follolwal recital:

> His Majesty King Victor Emmanuel III of Italy . . . and His Majesty Menelik II . . . desiring to settle definitively the frontier between the Italian possessions of Somalia and the provinces of the Ethiopian Empire, have determined to sign the following Convention:- . . .

The provisions of the Convention refer to 'the line of frontier between the Italian possessions of Somalia and the provinces of the Ethiopian Empire': see Article I. It is abundantly clear that the agreement is based upon the view that a partition of territories has taken place on the basis of the sovereignty of the two States over those territories. The Convention will be considered further and later in relation to its other legal consequences. It is referred to in the present context only on the basis that, valid or not, it provides *evidence* of the attitude of the States concerned on the issue of sovereignty.

(f) General Observations on the Legal Significance of the Treaties of the Period 1896-1908.

The general character and the precise provisions of the Treaties reviewed in the preceding paragraphs constitute strong evidence to the effect that, whatever the significance of the original treaties of protec-

tion concluded with the individual Somali tribes, the Powers had converted their initial influence and 'protection' into a territorial partition in which the legal personality of the tribes on the international plane became submerged. The Somali Tribes were not parties to the various agreements, although they are referred to in certain provisions as a part of the 'subject matter' of the agreements. Nor are the agreements made conditional upon the consent of the Somali Tribes to the territorial arrangements envisaged.

So far as the individual treaties are concerned, including the Anglo-Ethiopian Treaty of 1897, there are certain legally viable arguments to the effect that the treaties of the period 1896-1908 were incompatible with the earlier Treaties of Protection concluded with the Somali Tribes. On this basis, and perhaps on other legal grounds, the legal validity of the later agreements might be challenged. It is not intended to examine these arguments in depth, because in my opinion the legal position does not depend exclusively upon this issue. Certainly it is of moral and political significance that the Governments of Great Britain and Italy were prepared to renege on their undertakings to the Tribes, not least in ignoring their legal personality in subsequent dealings. However, there is a variety of evidence, a pattern of concordant material, establishing that in the years 1896-1908, and perhaps earlier, the British and Italian interest in the territories within their Protectorates amounted to territorial sovereignty: by usurpation and consolidation the possessions had been converted into colonial protectorates. Not only by means of particular treaties but by their general and consistent pattern of conduct from 1896 onward the States concerned expressly recognized, acquiesced in, their respective assertions of sovereignty over what had become colonial possessions. Thus, even if the legal validity of particular treaties were in question, the general recognition by conduct would remain. After the treaties of 1896 and 1897 (and setting them on on side) Great Britain, Italy and Ethiopia accepted by their conduct that the question of *frontiers* remained to be settled. The existence of a partition, a territorial settlement involving exclusive division between those three Powers (and France in the northern region), was assumed.

One finds it necessary to underline the considerations set forth in the previous paragraph. In the first place recognition by conduct of legal situations, of facts with certain legal consequences, is a part, and an important part, of international law. Secondly, all the evidence on a given issue has to be taken together. Thirdly, the legal consequences of events and conduct have to be assessed in the context of international law *as it existed at the material time*. This is the well-known principle of the inter-temporal law, stated by Judge Huber in the *Island of Palmas* case, Hague Court Reports, II, p. 83 at p. 100; and see also Jennings, *The Acquisition of Territory in International Law*, 1963, pp. 28-31; Waldock, *British Year Book of International Law*, Vol. 25 (1948), pp. 320-1; Fitzmaurice, *ibid*. Vol. 30 (1953), pp. 5-8.

The consolidation of colonial titles in East Africa in accordance with the complaisant international law of that period is in no way inimical to the application of the legal principle of self-determination, which is a feature of *contemporary* public international law. It is also appropriate to point out that the *decolonisation* of 1960 of parts of Somalia was a necessary consequence of pre-existing colonial titles. Likewise certain Somali official publications risk a certain contradiction since they produce arguments of fact and law to suggest the continued existence of the pre-colonial *status quo* whilst at the same time outlining the partition politics of the late nineteenth century and emphasising (with every justification) Ethiopia's major role in the colonisation of the Somali regions.

8. The significance of the 1908 Treaty in International Law

This agreement appears, in an English translation, in *British and Foreign State Papers*, Vol. 101, p. 1000. It is entitled 'Convention between Ethiopia and Italy settling the Frontier between the Italian Possessions of Somaliland and the Ethiopian Empire'. In certain official Somali publications arguments have been advanced to the effect that this instrument lacked legal validity on the ground that it was incompatible with prior obligations under Treaties of Protection and on other grounds: see *The Portion of Somali Territory under Ethiopian Colonization*, 1974, p. 21; *The Somali Peoples' Quest for Unity*, 1965, p. 13. Without adopting the view that such arguments lack substance, one would respectfully suggest that such arguments are not entirely in point.

The legal and evidential propositions set forth above are relevant here also. The 1908 Treaty did not exist in isolation, in some sort of vacuum. It was preceded by a pattern of evidence to the effect that a partition of territory had occurred. Even if the Treaty of 1908 be ignored, as invalid, or as impossible to implement and therefore terminated subsequently, the States concerned, and States generally from 1908 until the era of the United Nations Charter, adopted the territorial status quo, *subject only to*:-

(a) the need to demarcate the Anglo-Ethiopian boundary subsequent to the 1897 Treaty; and

(b) the need to resolve the dispute concerning the interpretation and application of the 1908 Treaty as between Ethiopia and Italy.

In the period between 1908 and, say, 1942 or 1945, States generally and also Ethiopia, Great Britain and Italy acted upon the basis that no area existed which was either under independent Somali rule or *terra nullius* and therefore open to acquisition by any State. In numerous instances States by their conduct indicated their adoption *as a general principle* of the territorial settlement resulting from the treaties of 1896-1908. This adoption or recognition of the *outcome* of those treaties provides an independent basis in international law for the territorial settlement, apart from the treaties themselves: in other words, whatever the legal status of the treaties *qua* treaties.

A great deal of map evidence indicates that, apart from the uncertainty attending the Ethiopian – Italian Somaliland boundary, the region was *exclusively parcelled out*. A substantial area might be in dispute – but only on the basis that it was either under Italian or under Ethiopian sovereignty. As an early example of the map evidence, see the following official British map:

Abyssinia, 1:3,000,000. Topographical Section. General Staff, No. 2319; War Office 1908.

This map is inscribed 'provisional issue only', but has considerable significance nonetheless, since it coincides with the end of the era of partition in East Africa.

The diplomatic material generated by the famous Wal-Wal incident of 1934 and the Italian war of annexation of 1935-36 gives no support to the view that the territorial settlement of 1896-1908 was voidable or incomplete. The general reaction to Italian expansionist tendencies and military aggression was to assume that *all* territory was attributable *either* to Italy *or* to Ethiopia and to make efforts to ascertain what the actual frontier should be.

Modern studies of the boundary issue present findings in line with the evidence outlined so far: see, for example, International Boundary Study, United States Department of State, Bureau of Intelligence and Research, The Geographer, No. 153, Ethiopia-Somalia Boundary, 5 November, 1975.

It is now possible to examine the ramifications of the actual provisions of the 1908 Treaty. As is well known the attempt to demarcate the line described failed and only some 30 kilometres were marked by an Ethiopian-Italian Boundary Commission in 1910-11. One does not consider it appropriate to review the complex and extensive evidential matter concerning the dispute over the interpretation of the provisions of the 1908 Treaty: in any case such an examination would involve a substantial project in itself. Nor is it considered necessary to do more than advance the thesis that, on the evidence, the provisions are so substantially and irredeemably obscure that the 1908 Treaty at some point was revealed to be impossible of execution. For the present purpose it will suffice to report on the dimensions of the dispute in terms of the contentions of interested Governments at various times. As sources of information one has drawn on the following items: *The Somali Peninsula*, 1962, pp. 59-60; Memorandum transmitted by the Ethiopian Government to the United Nations, U.N. Doc. A/3502, 17 January, 1957; Report of the Ethiopian Government, U.N. Doc. A/3753, 27 November 1957; Report of the Ethiopian Government, UN Doc. A/4323, 3 December, 1959.

The principal, but by no means the only, permutations of view concerning the line prescribed by the 1908 Treaty are as follows:-

(a) A line 180 miles from the coast, from the Dolo sector in the west to a tripoint with British Somaliland at longitude 47°E, latitude 8°N;

(b) A line 180 miles from the coast but in the northern sector deflected to the east to reach a tripoint with British Somaliland at longitude 48°E, latitude 8°N;

(c) A line commencing at Dolo and passing via Lugh to Baidoa, thence approximately at a distance of 140 miles from the coast as far as the British Somaliland tripoint at longitude 48°E, latitude 8°N;

(d) A line at a distance of 140 miles from the sea commencing at Bardera on the River Giuba in the west and passing northwards to the British Somaliland tripoint at longitude 48°E, latitude 8°N.

(e) A line (substantially that of the British provisional administrative line of 1950) commencing at Dolo and winding eastwards as far as the Uebi Scebeli (River) to the north of Belet Uen and then passing northwards approximately at a distance of 140 miles from the coast until the British Somaliland tripoint is reached at longitude 48°E, latitude 8°N.

This analytical survey of the permutations of claim based upon the 1908 Treaty and the other relevant evidence such as maps and unilateral declarations, leads to a firm and unavoidable conclusion: on the maximum view of what was in issue, and on any view of the matter which could be reasonably adopted, the territory in issue was a band roughly situated between the line Bardera – British Somaliland tripoint at 48°E longitude and a line from Dolo in the west to a tripoint with British Somaliland at 47°E longitude. This constitutded a very substantial territorial dispute: but it had nothing to do with pushing Ethiopia back to her traditional pre-colonial frontiers. The original boundary of the Somali country was not in issue. The region presently described as

Western Somalia was not in dispute, except in part and then only incidentally in the context of the Italo-Ethiopian dispute.

At the time of independence Somalia in principle inherited the Italian boundary (for what it was worth) and thus inherited the dispute. *This dispute is a distinct question from the issue of the legal status of Western Somalia as a unit of self-determination.* Technically the dispute is about the interim question of how much territory was decolonised by Italy in 1960: it is in a sense a preliminary issue to the decolonisation of Western Somalia. Obviously, in reality and as a logical consequence, the ultimate and predominant question of the status of Western Somalia is seen, or is assumed, to render the boundary issue theoretical and redundant.

Thus the boundary dispute, being a distinct issue logically and legally, is not incompatible with the position taken by the Somali Government on the issue of self-determination. Thus when the observation is made that the issue with Ethiopia 'is not a frontier question' this is true in two senses:

(a) the predominant, the overriding issue, is that of the status of Western Somalia;

(b) on the assumption that Western Somalia, when free to do so, opts for union with the rest of Somalia the frontier question lapses.

At the same time in a strict sense the issues do include the frontier question, and in one form the boundary issue does interact with the question of self-determination. Thus the concept of Western Somalia as 'a unit of self-determination' does involve a national separate parcel contingent upon union with Somalia. By the same logic involving the principle of self-determination, on the hypothesis that Western Somalia did not opt for union, the alignment would, of course, survive as an international boundary.

9. Attitude of Governments to the dispute concerning the 1908 Treaty in the period 1950 to 1960

From the point of view of international law it is necessary to record some more or less negative assessments of the behaviour of the various Governments prior to the partial decolonisation of Somalia in 1960.

In 1941 the British Government established a 'provisional administrative line' separating the territory of Italian Somaliland (placed under belligerent occupation prior to a Peace Treaty) and the territory of Ethiopia liberated from Italian rule and reconstituted, on the legal basis that the Italian conquest had been a nullity and there was a continuity of Ethiopian statehood. In 1950 this 'provisional administrative line' was the object of a description contained in a letter to the President of the

44

Trusteeship Council from the Permanent United Kingdom Representative on the Council: see Appendix 13. The letter states that the arrangement 'is a provisional one only and without prejudice to the final settlement of this question'. Thus the British Government did not by its actions preclude any issue of legal rights.

The attitude of Italy as Administering Power, by virtue of the United Nations Trusteeship in respect of the former Italian colony, is of some interest. In principle the Italian Government could not make any disposition or act in any manner which would preclude the boundary issues. In international law an Administering Power has no competence to make dispositions affecting the frontiers of the Trusteeship territory without the authority or consent of the United Nations. Moreover, there is no evidence that the Italian Government purported to change the *status quo*.

The negotiations between Ethiopia and Italy in the period 1955-59 under the auspices of the United Nations have some significance, though not as much as might be expected. The negotiations provided a forum for the public statement of positions on the interpretation of the 1908 Treaty. Nothing was in fact settled. However, there was one development of some interest within the framework of the present text. During the negotiations of 1959 for the purpose of drafting a *Compromis* for the constitution of an Arbitration Tribunal, the Italian Government adopted a different approach to that of the Ethiopian side: see UN Gen. Ass., Official Records, 14th Sess., Agenda Item 40, Annexes, A/4323 and A/4324. The Italian amendments to the draft *Compromis* were intended to empower the Arbitration Tribunal 'to decide *ex aequo et bono*, as if in the matter in question the Tribunal were legislator'. From this and other evidence it is clear that the Italian Government had come to appreciate that the issues had a wider ambit than the technical problems of treaty interpretation: see in particular UN Doc. A/4323, paragraph 7.

There is one other matter worth brief notice. During the proceedings in the Trusteeship Council concerning the progress towards independence of Italian Somaliland no reference was made to the association of that issue and the future of Western Somalia. It has to be concluded that, in the practice of the United Nations and the Member States *in the period prior to 1960*, Western Somalia was not envisaged as a unit of self-determination. At the same time nothing had occurred which would constitute an absolute bar to such a determination in the future.

10. The Principle of Self-Determination as recognised in modern International Law

The chronological and analytical evolution of this text has reached a stage which can be described as follows:

(a) The colonial partition, in which Ethiopia participated, has submerged the legal personality of the individual Tribes of the pre-colonial Somali country;

(b) The partition has been recognized, adopted and confirmed by the treaties of the period 1896-1908 and in other ways by the conduct of the states concerned and of other states.

(c) The unresolved Ethiopian – Italian dispute concerning the 1908 Treaty neither presented nor precluded the general question of the status of Western Somalia;

(d) In 1960 decolonisation of the British Protectorate and the Trust Territory of Somalia took place, a process which was not extended to Western Somalia.

After achieving independence in 1960 the Government of Somalia immediately set about a programme for achieving the unity of the Somali nation under one flag. In doing so the principle of self-determination was invoked and it is now appropriate to examine the legal aspects of this principle.

Since 1945 the principle of self-determination has been recognised as a *legal* concept. The key development was the appearance of references to 'the principle of equal rights and self-determination of peoples' in Article 1(2), Article 55, and Articles 73-74, of the Charter of the United Nations. The principle has been confirmed by the practice of the Member States expressed through the organs of the United Nations: see Rosalyn Higgins, *The Development of International Law Through the Political Organs of the United Nations*, 1963, pp. 90-106; Whiteman, *Digest of International Law*, Vol. V, Dept. of State Publication 7873, release June 1965, pp. 66-83; *Repertory of Practice of United Nations Organs*, Vol. III, 1955, Chap. IX, paras. 220-25; the same, suppl. No. 1, Vol. II, 1958, Chap. IX, paras. 91-92; the same, Suppl. No. 2, Vol. III, 1963, Chap. IX. paras. 114-18; the same, Suppl. No. 3, Vol. II; 1971, Chap. IX, paras. 176-78; A Rigo Sureda, *The Evolution of the Right of Self-Determination*, Leiden, 1973, *passim*.

The General Assembly has affirmed the principle in a series of resolutions which have probative value as a form of subsequent practice of the parties to the Charter: and subsequent practice is a well accepted aid to the interpretation of treaties. In Resolution 637 A(vii) of 16 December, 1952, the General Assembly recommended, *inter alia*, that 'the State Members of the United Nations shall uphold the principle of self-determination of all peoples and nations'. Of particular significance is the Declaration on the Granting of Independence to Colonial Countries and Peoples adopted by the General Assembly in 1960, see Appendix 14 and referred to in a series of resolutions concerning specific territories. The Declaration regards the principle of self-determination as a part of the obligations for States stemming from the Charter. The Declaration does not employ the language of recommendation, but is in the form of an authoritive interpretation of the Charter: see Judge Sir Humphrey Waldock, *Recueil des Cours*, Hague Academy of International Law, Vol. 106 (1962, II), at pp. 33-34; Annual Report of the Secretary-General (1961), p. 2. See further Whiteman, *Digest of International Law*, Vol. XIII, Dept. of State Publication 8424, released December 1968, pp. 701-68. The voting on the resolution containing the Declaration was 89 to nil, with 9 abstentions. Abstentions were not necessarily based upon opposition to the principle of the Resolution: see the US explanation of vote, Off. Records, General Assembly, 15th Sess. (Part I), Plen. Meetings, Vol. 2, 947th Plen. Meeting, 14 Dec. 1960, paras. 142-154.

The principle of self-determination has been incorporated in the two Covenants adopted by the General Assembly in 1966: see the International Covenant on Civil and Political Rights, Article 1(1); and the International Covenant on Economic, Social and Cutural Rights, Article 1(1). This paragraph provides as follows:

All peoples have the right to self-determination. By virtue of that right they freely determine their political status and freely pursue their economic, social and cultural development.

The United States supports the principle: see the statement in U.N. General Assembly, 12 October 1966, *Dept. of State Bulletin*, Vol. 55, p. 690; *American Journal of International Law*, Vol. 61 (1967), p. 595, and previously. Indeed, the principle is recognized by most governments. The most recent multilateral act of recognition is the Declaration of Principles of International Law concerning Friendly Relations adopted by the General Assembly in 1970: Resolution 2625(XXV), Annex (Text: *American Journal*, Vol. 65 (1971), p. 243). See Appendix 16.

The Resolution 'approves the Declaration' and was accepted as a Consensus, i.e. without a vote.

In conclusion, it is submitted that the principle of self-determination is part of international law and no longer merely a political desideratum. This view would be inevitably adopted by authoritative decison makers and tribunals. Thus it plays a major role in the reasoning of the Advisory Opionion of October 16, 1975, concerning the status of the *Western Sahara*: I.C.J. Reports, 1975, p. 12. The material passages of the majority Opinion are at pp. 29-33 (paras. 48-59) See Appendix 17.

Certain general pronouncements on the principle of self-determination, stressing that it applies to all non-self-governing territories, appear also in the Advisory Opinion on *Legal Consequences for States of the Continued Presence of South Africa in Namibia Notwithstanding Security Council Resolution 276 (1970)*, I.C.J. Reports, 1971, p. 16 at pp. 30-31 (paras. 50-52).

11. The application of the principle of Self-Determination to the people of Western Somalia and the concept of a Unit of Self-Determination

Two questions of principle must be resolved. The first concerns the argument that self-determination only applies to 'classical colonialism', involving extra-regional domination, often referred to as the 'salt water theory'. The second issue involves the determination whether Western Somalia constitutes a 'unit of self-determination'.

The criteria for 'a unit of self-determination' are stated in Principle IV of the Annex to Resolution 1541 (XV) (see Appendix 15). The criteria may be formulated as follows: a non-self-governing people is the permanent population of a territory 'which is geographically separate and is distinct ethically and/or culturally from the country administering it'. One is of the firm opinion that the principle of self-determination is not confined to 'overseas' colonial situations of the kind familiar in Africa and Asia.

In the first place the Somali country is, in fact, geographically separate from Ethiopia and, in particular, the lowlands are distinct in character from the Shoan Highlands.

Secondly, the application of the principle of self-determination in the practice of United Nations organs has not been precluded by the claim by the colonial power that the territory concerned was a *part* (in some constitutional law sense) of France, Portugal or Spain.

Thirdly, and most importantly, the wording of the key resolution, General Assembly Resolution 1514 of 1960 (Appendix 14) the normative and legal source of self-determination in modern international law, by no means restricts the principle to overseas possessions. The Declaration contained in Resolution 1514 (see paragraph 2) refers to 'all *peoples*', (emphasis supplied): and the preambular part (second *considerandum*) also refers to 'all peoples'. Paragraph 5 of the Declaration refers to 'Trust and Non-Self-Governing Territories *or all other ter-*

ritories which have not yet attained independence' (emphasis supplied).

The literature of international law concerning self-determination contains certain expressions of the opinion that the principle 'has been restricted to colonial situations': see A. Rigo Sureda, *The Evolution of the Right of Self-Determination*, Leiden, 1973, p. 106. It seems that such expressions of opinion are unreliable. In the first place, granted that until the late nineteen sixties United Nations practice had been almost exclusively concerned with the independence of colonies in the classical sense, it does not follow that in normative terms the principle of self-determination is restricted a certain formations. Secondly, since 1965 there has been a growth of United Nations practice (and therefore the practice of States generally participating in United Nations organs) involving the clear application of self-determination outside the colonial agenda. This recent appearance of 'bridge' cases is of enormous importance to the position of Western Somalia.

The episodes (not all closed of course) which have involved self-determination outside the normal colonial/overseas possessions model include the following:-

(a) *Rhodesia after the Unilateral Declaration of Independence in 1965.* Although formally the United Kingdom retained its role as administering power, *de facto* Rhodesia was no longer a colony of the United Kingdom. At no stage was this change considered to affect the right of self-determination of the people of Zimbabwe/Rhodesia as a whole.

(b) *United Nations resolutions relating to Palestine in the period after the 1967 war.* In particular, General Assembly Resolution 2672 (XXV) of 8 December 1970, 'recognizes that the people of Palestine are entitled to equal rights and self-determination, in accordance with the Charter of the United Nations'; and see also Resolution 2787 (XXVI) of 6 December 1971. The recognition that the Palestinian people have 'legitimate rights' to a 'homeland' is universal and lately even the United States has adopted this view: see a recent US-Soviet Joint Declaration.

(c) *The response of the international community to the secession of Bangla Desh (East Bengal) from Pakistan in 1971.* This episode is of considerable interest. Given the nature of East Bengal as a society, and given the domination of East Bengal by West Pakistan, States generally were prepared to treat the case as an application of the principle of self-determination *in spite of* the role of Indian intervention in preventing Pakistan from reasserting her control. The United Nations General Assembly simply called for a cease-fire (Resolution 2793 (XXVI), 7 December, 1971) and in due course all Members of the international community recognised the new State.

The conclusion which is inescapable is that the practice of States (the source of customary international law) subsequent to Resolution 1514 of 1960 serves to confirm the view that the Resolution, and the principle which it embodies, is not confined to the self-determination of overseas possessions, i.e. extra-regional domination.

The final stage of the enquiry is to consider the application to the people of Western Somalia of the criteria other than that of geographical separateness. Principle IV of the Annex to Resolution 1541 (XV) prescribes as follows: 'which is geographically separate and is distinct ethnically and/or culturally from the country administering it'. Whilst it is a question of appreciation, the application of the legal criteria of a unit of self-determination to the authoritative description of Somali society set forth in the works of numerous scholars and eminent lawyers leads, and can only lead, to one conclusion. *The Somali people possess, conspicuously and decisively, the characteristics of being ethnically and culturally distinct and separate from other peoples of the region.* The Somali would seem to qualify in these terms at least as much as other groups which have been accorded the right of self-determination.

The assessment of the Somali people as a whole – and consequently of the people of Western Somalia as a distinct group remaining under foreign rule – and a unit of self-determination is corroborated by the important evidence considered earlier concerning the pre-colonial reality of the Somali country, outside the recognized frontiers of Ethiopia and shown on contemporary maps as Somali-Land, having its own character and homogeneity: (see, by way of an example the important map published by W. and A.K. Johnston in 1885).

In concluding the consideration of the issues relating to the principle of self-determination in its legal aspects, it is necessary to point out that, given the capacity of a unit for self-determination, it is recognized that the *exercise* of the right may take three forms:- (a) emergence as a sovereign independent State; (b) free association with an independent State; or, (c) integration with an independent State (see Resolution 1541 (XV), Annex, Principle VI).

12. The relevance of the Charter of the Organisation of African Unity

The Charter of the O.A.U. was adopted by a conference of Heads of States and Governments in Addis Ababa on 25 May, 1963. A convenient text is to be found in Brownlie (ed.), *Basic Documents in International Law*, 2nd ed., 1972, p. 68. The provisions of Article III are, so far as material, as follows:

'The Member States, in pursuit of the purposes stated in Article 2, solemnly affirm and declare their adherence to the following principles: . . .

3. Respect for the sovereignty and territorial integrity of each State and for its inalienable right to independent existence.'

This Article is sometimes referred to as having the effect of freezing the *status quo* so far as boundaries and other territorial issues are concerned, but the provision could not have that consequence. Such a provision is a common form for the expression of obligations not to resort to physical interference, and principally not to resort to the use of armed force, directed against other States. Such a provision by no means rules out the existence and presentation of claims based upon legal considerations. Moreover, the term 'territorial integrity' involves a standard of conduct, a duty not to disturb the *status quo* in a physical sense. The term is completely question-begging in relation to frontier and other territorial issues since 'territorial integrity' assumes that the object concerned is ascertained.

13. The legal effects of the Cairo Resolution of 21 July 1964

At the Cairo Assembly of Heads of State and Government of the O.A.U., 17-21 July, 1964, the following General Resolution on Border Disputes was adopted:

'The Assembly of Heads of State and Government . . .

1. *Solemnly reaffirms* the strict respect by all Member States of the Organization for the principles laid down in paragraph 3 of Article III of the Charter of the Organization of African Unity;

2. *Solemnly declares* that all Member States pledge themselves to respect the borders existing on their achievement of national independence.'

The interpretation and legal effect of this Resolution are matters of the first importance, both legally and politically. It is far from easy to consult the O.A.U. Mimeographed text. However, the following materials have been consulted: *Assembly of the Heads of State and Government of the O.A.U., Speeches Delivered at the Assembly, Cairo, 17-21 July 1964*, Information Department. U.A.R., and Touval, *International Organization*, Vol. 21 (1967), pp. 102-127 (a well documented account).

The Resolution did not constitute a treaty. However, consent may be given in other ways. States voting for the Resolution or subsequently adopting it by means of their declarations of intention and other conduct would become bound by the principles stated in the instrument (*subject to the effect of Article 103* of the United Nations Charter, on which see further below). In any event Somalia did not accept the

Resolution: see *The Somali Republic and the Organization of African Unity*, pp. 16-24; and Touval, *op. cit.*, at p. 124. The matter does not end there, however, since the issues involve the effect of the Resolution in terms of Somalia's relations with other States, including Ethiopia, which have adopted the Resolution. Thus its interpretation remains a matter affecting Somalia.

The *travaux préparatoires* of the Resolution are not particularly helpful. Nevertheless, the general purpose was to affirm that the fact of decolonization did not place frontiers in issue. The *status quo* was to be preserved: and this necessarily involved the continuance of existing legal disputes, since the legal *status quo* includes outstanding issues and uncertainties. Similarly, the Resolution did not apply to pre-colonial issues such as the dispute between Algeria and Morocco.

The text does not explicity state that it does not apply to 'old' disputes, but that is of little significance. 'Existing borders' can only refer to alignments which have been established as definitive boundaries.

The position adopted in the previous paragraph is confirmed in two ways. In the first place since 1964 a substantial proportion of Member States of the O.A.U. have raised, and sometimes settled, frontier disputes, and issues of demarcation, without meeting a plea of inadmissibility by reason of the Cairo Resolution. Secondly, similar principles which have been adopted in Latin America and Asian regional state practice have always been understood to involve the assumption that maintenance of the colonial *status quo* did not involve an automatic avoidance of legal disputes concerning boundaries. In Central and South America the doctrine of *uti possidetis juris* has been adopted: see Hyde, *International Law Chiefly as Interpreted and Applied by the United States*, 2nd ed., 1945, I, pp. 498-510; Brownlie, *Principles of Public International Law*, 2nd ed., 1973, pp. 137-8. The principle of *uti possidetis juris* is a part of regional international law and bases territorial settlements upon a rule of presumed possession by the former Spanish administrative units. Asian Governments have adopted a policy similar to that of the O.A.U.: see, in particular, the *Temple* case, I.C.J. Reports, 1962, p. 6; and the *Rann of Kutch Arbitration*, International Law Reports (Ed. E. Lauterpacht), Vol. 50, p. 2.

The conclusion must be that issues existing when the Cairo Resolution was adopted are not precluded by it at least when the issues concern frontiers as such. Thus the issues concerning the 1908 Treaty are unaffected. A more difficult question to resolve is the relation between the Cairo Resolution and issues arising from the principle of self-determination. There is a quantity of evidence in the speeches delivered at Cairo which suggests that the Resolution was probably intended to exclude changes urged on ethnic and linguistic grounds. However, it could be argued that the Resolution was not expressly concerned with the legal status of 'units of self-determination', a question which goes well beyond the category of 'border disputes', and is qualitatively distinct.

A further point may be taken. The principle of self-determination is also a part of the principles of the United Nations Charter. Article 103 of the United Nations Charter provides as follows:

In the event of a conflict between the obligations of the Members of the United Nations under the present Charter and their obligations under any other international agreement, *their obligations under the present Charter shall prevail.*

In so far as the Cairo Resolution is an interpretation and application of the O.A.U. Charter, which is, of course, an international agreement, Article 103 must apply. It is also the case that Article 103 applies on the basis that the Cairo Resolution constitutes an informal international agreement (not in treaty form).

14. Some pertinent Soviet practice

More for its diplomatic than legal significance, there is some Soviet state practice which is of relevance in the present context. After the collapse of Poland in September 1939 the USSR incorporated the Western Ukraine and Western Byelorussia into the Ukrainian SSR and Byelorussian SSR respectively. These changes were controversial in view of their background – the use of force against Poland. However, they had an undoubted ethnic basis and Soviet literature expressly invokes the principle of self-determination based upon plebiscites for union with Byelorussia and the Ukraine: see Kozhevnikov, *International Law*, Moscow, n.d. (*circa* 1960), pp. 185-6. For further documentation and information see: Degras, *Soviet Documents on Foreign Policy*, O.U.P., 1953, III, pp. 388-93; Umiastowski, *Poland, Russia and Great Britain, 1941-1945*, London, 1946; *Krushchev Remembers*, ed. by Crankshaw, 1971, pp. 118-22.

15. Conclusions

It is not intended to summarise all that has gone before by way of conclusion, but to select the key points for clarity and emphasis. There is no doubt that the relevant material could be studied with greater attention to detail and that more cartographic and documentary evidence is to be found. Thus the present view in relation to the material which is available and to the significance of the issues, is in some sense preliminary. At the same time it is believed that the principal legal issues and the main structure of the controversy have been presented.

The important features are as follows:

(a) Prior to the Menelik conquests of 1886-1892 the Somali country was neither *terra nullius* nor under Ethiopian sovereignty;

(b) Prior to 1884 and in the early years of the colonial period the individual Somali tribes kept their legal personality on the plane of international law;

(c) In the years 1896-1908, if not before, the Somali Country was subjected to an effective (in terms of international law) colonial partition, involving the submergence of the legal personality of the Somali tribes;

(d) Western Somalia qualifies as a unit of self-determination in modern international law, including the law of the United Nations;

(e) The issue of self-determination is distinct from and in a sense overrides any 'frontier' or 'territorial' dispute concerning titles *as between Ethiopia and Somalia*;

(f) The legal issues concerning the application of 1908 Treaty have been inherited by Somalia from the colonial predecessor;

(g) The issues concerning the 1908 Treaty are not incompatible with the issue of self-determination: technically they are distinct and are related to the *limits* of the unit of self-determination, Western Somalia, prior to the *exercise* of the right of self-determination;

(h) If, as a mere analytical hypothesis, Western Somalia were to opt for independence rather than union, then the new State would inherit the issues concerning the 1908 Treaty: this proposition merely serves to demonstrate the separate identity of the 'frontier issue';

(i) In so far as the Charter of the O.A.U., and the subsequent practice of the Member States, are incompatible with the principle of self-determination, the latter principle must prevail in accordance with the provisions of Article 103 of the United Nations Charter.

It would therefore appear that the important legal and political task is to establish the application of the principle of self-determination where appropriate outside the classical agenda of 'overseas' colonialism where pages 48 to 50 are relevant.

Overall it must be said that Western Somalia qualifies for the right to self-determination, and *there is an international duty to ensure that it is achieved.*

Note

(a) Treaties of 1896, 1897, 1905 and 1908 appear as Appendix 12

(b) UN Resolution 742 (VIII) appears as Appendix 18

(c) OAU Resolution AHG/Res 16 (I) appears as Appendix 19

Chapter 6

DUTY

Finally we come to the fundamental meaning of the word, and how it is to be understood. Duty is not concerned with something that *could* be done, nor does it embrace something that *should* be done; quite simply it means something that *must* be done.

Depending upon the status of the person responsible, a guiding principle is contained in the maxim *noblesse oblige* and what that may imply especially to those who by birth, merit or otherwise, have it in their power to administer the lives of their brother human beings. A random example can be taken from the British House of Lords when a question was asked: 'Whether, in view of our debt of honour and moral obligation to the Somalis arising from arrangements with Ethiopia (Abyssinia) between 1897 and 1954, they will instruct our Permanent Representative at the United Nations to raise the question of self-determination for Somalis in Ethiopia as a right to which they are entitled under the Charter (and numerous subsequent resolutions)?'

The reply given was: 'No. Our position is one of support for the Organisation of African Unity policy of accepting the colonial boundaries inherited by the newly-independent African states; indeed, it has been widely accepted at the United Nations that the right of self-determination does not give every distinct group or territorial sub-division within a state the right to secede from it and thereby dismember the territorial integrity or political unity of sovereign independent states.' (see: British House of Lords official record – Hansard – for 12 December 1983, cols 93 and 94).

It is, of course, for the reader to perceive that answer as he wishes, but I believe that it was completely inadequate.

This must pose a deeper question: will authority face up to, or will it not, the duties implicit within the responsibilities which it has accepted?

The outcome must be plain to see: those (whomsoever they may be) who are charged with the well-being of others as a duty, but yet see fit to

56

evade that duty, must condemn themselves to drown in the ocean of tears to which they have added by reason that very evasion.

If readers of this work find this a point worthy of ponder, so be it.

I slept, and dreamed that life was Beauty;
I woke, and found that life is Duty.

Ellen Sturgis Hooper 1816-1841
Beauty and Duty (1840)

APPENDICES

Appendix 1

UN DOCUMENT E/CN. 4/1503
31 DECEMBER 1981

QUESTION OF THE VIOLATION OF HUMAN RIGHTS AND
FUNDAMENTAL FREEDOMS IN ANY PART OF THE WORLD, WITH
PARTICULAR REFERENCE TO COLONIAL AND OTHER DEPENDENT
COUNTRIES AND TERRITORIES

Study on
Human Rights and Massive Exoduses

SADRUDDIN AGA KHAN
SPECIAL RAPPORTEUR

The suppressed information

The paragraphs of Annex II, dealing with Ethiopia and Eritrea and brutally honest
in their criticism of the Ethiopian government, deleted from the original UN Report
when reissued 'for technical reasons'.

26. In the seven years which have elapsed since a military takeover changed the
politial face of the Ethiopian empire and set it on the path of socialism, events
so devastating have occurred that millions of people have been internally displaced or have fled to surrounding countries.

27. Ethiopia's heterogeneous population of some 30 million people, belonging
to possibly as many as 75 ethnic groups, knew little change during the half century in which the late Emperor Haile Selassie dominated the largely feudal
empire-state. Ethiopia, its soil eroded after widespread deforestation, its peasants heavily taxed and having to battle for survival, was classified as one of the
10 least developed countries in the world. Despite the introduction of reforms
in education and the presence in foreign universities of large numbers of Ethiopian students for whom places in the national university did not suffice, an estimated 95 per cent of the adult population remained illiterate. While a leading
role in the Organization of African Unity was assumed by the then Emperor,
Ethiopia's own political life largely stagnated. In 1974, years of mounting

61

Letter of transmission which accompanied the Special Rapporteur's report

Sir,

In accordance with paragraph 7 of Resolution 29 (XXXVII) of your Commission, I have the honour to submit herewith the Study on Massive Exoduses and Human Rights.

It is a modest attempt at dealing succinctly with a colossal and increasingly complex problem. The phenomenon of mass exodus, which is becoming a tragically permanent feature of our times, owes its existence to a variety of aspects inherent in contemporary society, each of which calls for an independent and detailed study of its own. The problem is bound to become more serious with time unless imaginative and concrete measures are urgently taken to contain, if not avert, situations of mass exodus. A prerequisite for such measures is the political will of governments, translated into reality at global level.

If the present Study serves only to increase the awareness of the problem by governments and the general public, and provides an incentive for the matter to be further analysed, it will not have been in vain. It is, however, my considered opinion that if we are to succeed in any measure to spare future generations the spectre of millions of uprooted people, more is required than reports and resolutions, however pertinent and useful they may be.

In concluding, I am reminded of what George Bernanos wrote in one of his essays,

"A thought which does not result in an action is nothing much, and an action which does not proceed from a thought is nothing at all."

Accept, Sir, the assurances of my highest consideration.

Sadruddin Aga Khan

His Excellency
Mr Carlos Callero Rodrigues
Ambassador
Chairman, Commission on Human Rights
United Nations Office at Geneva
Palais des Nations
1211 Geneva 10

APPENDIX 1

TABLE OF CONTENTS

Above: the Table of Contents which appeared in the original report.
Below: the Table of Contents of the re-issued report.

TABLE OF CONTENTS

unrest epitomized by the gathering momentum of the student movement were capped by general indignation at the inertia of the imperial government at a time of severe famine in Wollo and Tigre provinces which took a very heavy toll of lives. A revolutionary situation rapidly evolved which culminated in the gradual overthrow of the old regime by the armed forces and police, supported by the intelligentsia.

28. The new military administration was to tackle tasks of revolutionizing the political, economic and social structures of the vast and disparate country in the face of major insurrections in the north and south east and a maelstrom of religious, tribal and ideological battles. Disruption of the economy resulting from the drafting of very substantial numbers of men into the army and People's Militia, from acts of sabotage or of war, from drought conditions and from locust infestation exacerbated conditions in the young socialist state.

Forces were set in motion which internationalized some of the conflict and had serious repercussions for Ethiopia and its neighbours, Djibouti, Somalia and the Sudan in particular.

Some estimates of the numbers displaced within Ethiopia or across its borders put them as high as six million.

29. Under the influence of left-wing intellectuals returning from abroad, the Provisional Military Administrative Council – PMAC, popularly known as the Dergue – in December 1974 declared Ethiopia a socialist state, nationalized or took over partial control of over a hundred companies and shortly afterwards nationalized all rural land. It took the decision to despatch tens of thousands of students to rural areas where they were charged with carrying out health and literacy education and to help organize the land reform measures, including the establishment of peasant associations intended ultimately to organize themselves into co-operatives and communal farms. Their counterpart in the towns were urban dwellers' associations or *kebeles*, which shortly took took on the tasks of local government under the Dergue.

30. Those dedicated to revolution in Ethiopia were by no means all attuned to the same ideological line, nor was the Dergue free from internal rivalries. Of two prominent parties, Me-ei Sone (or Meison), which was communist/soviet oriented, favoured the continuation of military rule for the time being, with the support of Lt-Col Mengistu, while the other, the Ethiopian People's Revolutionary Party (EPRP), which had published its programme first and argued for the establishment of a people's civilian government as well as independence for Eritrea, fell into disfavour. From September 1976 onwards, the Dergue and Me-ei Sone carried out a campaign against their opponents which was the more intense for acts of urban terrorism the EPRP was promoting. Widespread killings and mass arrests marked the period from November 1977 to mid-1978, when chiefs of *kebeles* were publicly asked by Mengistu to sow 'red terror' against opponents of the government, particularly the EPRP. If that party was the first casualty, Me-ei Sone, increasingly critical of the Dergue, found its own leaders having to go underground. Large numbers of young

Amharas fled the country. Meanwhile, the Head of State and several other top members of the Dergue were eliminated and Lt-Col Mengistu emerged as the new Chairman of the PMAC and Head of State. A few months later, Lt-Col Atnafu, the Vice-Chairman, was removed.

31. The Dergue and its politburo, the Provisional Office of Mass Organizational Affairs (POMOA) had to address themselves to the question of what measures of autonomy could be granted to the country's main ethnic groupings, about a dozen of which could be called major nationalities.

The question lay at the crux of the country's future. Traditionally, the Amharas, a Christian people of the central highland provinces of Shoa, Gojam, Begemder and Wollo, had wielded power, and after Emperor Menilik II had undertaken military campaigns to conquer or re-conquer territories which now made up some of Ethiopia's 14 regions, lands were increasingly bestowed upon Amhara people as marks of favour. The inhabitants of many of those regions considered themselves a distinct people, with their own language, culture and, for the most part, a different religion from the Coptic Christian faith of the Amharas. In particular, the Oromos, a numerically important group, the Eritreans, the Somalis and the Tigreans found cause to fight for varying degrees of autonomy against first the imperial administrations, then the much more centralized authority of a new socialist state largely governed by Amharas, whose language had been made the official language of the country.

32. Eritrea, the coastal region on the Red Sea which possesses two strategic points at Massawa and Assab, had already been torn by conflict since 1962, when the former Italian colony which claimed a long history of its own was, despite the 1950 resolution of the UN General Assembly which gave it a federated status with Ethiopia, incorporated into the Empire by Haile Selassie. The rebellion, mounted by factions which did not always see eye to eye, did not pose too serious a threat to the authorities in Addis Ababa until, after about 17 years, their position was favoured by events in eastern Ethiopia which drew much of the national army to the Ogaden.

Nevertheless, there had been a steady stream of refugees from Eritrea into Sudan throughout most of those years, as the ability to sustain life at home was eroded by the ongoing conflict.

At the beginning of 1978, the Eritrean movements were in the strongest military position they had enjoyed so far. It took a major onslaught, mounted in May 1978 after the last main towns of the Ogaden had been recaptured by Addis Ababa, to break the back of the resistance. After the first few violent clashes, Mengistua broadcast on 7 June 1978 an offer of amnesty to those Eritrean guerrillas who surrendered peacefully and were willing to 'struggle for the triumph of the revolution'. On the same occasion he gave official figures of the toll of the Eritrean war to date: 13,000 soldiers and between 30,000 and 50,000 civilians killed or wounded; 200,000 people forced into exile; extensive damage to property and an estimated cost of pursuing the war of 2,500 million Birr or $1,200 million.

33. Whereas the leader of the Eritrean People's Liberation Front (EPFL) on 14 June 1978 stated that his movement rejected all peaceful solutions to the Eritrean issue, further massive military gains by Ethiopian forces rapidly caused a change of mind by both major Eritrean movements, but it was too late. The Ethiopian Chief Administrator of the region, Col Fikru Wolde Tensae, asserted that 'efforts for a peaceful solution have been exhausted', and that the secessionists now had to be taught 'a lesson they will never forget'. The Dergue on 14 July firmly rejected the EPLF-ELF (Eritrean Liberation Front) joint peace bid, labelling it a 'propaganda manoeuvre' and pledging to crush the separatists by force.* The war therefore continued with renewed intensity. Large areas of the region became desolate; their civilian population, believing their lives to be in jeopardy, fled towards the Sudan.

34. Although resistance has not been eliminated altogether, it has been sufficiently weakened for it to be restricted to the rural areas. The region has meanwhile been quite seriously affected by drought as a result of the failure of the 1980/81 winter rains. Malnutrition, already endemic in much of rural Eritrea as a result of centuries of ingrained poverty and the effects of the war, increasingly created conditions for the unchecked spread of disease. At the same time, under the martial law still in force, there is reported to be a continuing pattern of widespread arrests, torture and summary execution of those suspected of harbouring sympathies with the secessionist movements, and although the exodus from the region has dwindled since the height of the war, it has not yet stopped.

35. The Government has faced armed opposition from other quarters, notably in the provinces of Tigre, Begemder. Wollo, Hararghe, Bale and Sidamo, the last three encompassing the region known as the Ogaden. Conflict in the Ogaden arose from issues reaching far back into the history of the Horn of Africa. Ecologically and economically an integral part of the grazing lands of the Somali peoples with their Oromo (Galla) cousins, its international borders delineated by colonial powers recognized by the Government of Somalia only on a *de facto* basis, it had already given birth in the era of Haile Selassie to the Western Somali Liberation Front (WSLF), WSLF, expressing aspirations centuries old such as the right to practise transhumance across a vast area now divided by an internationally-recognized national boundary and so foster common loyalties much older than those now imposed by circumstances, engaged in an armed conflict into which Somalia entered in mid-1977. The eight-month war which ensued was as intense as any seen in that part of Africa. After it ended, the chief administrator of Hararghe, Commander Lemma Gutema, stated that 70 per cent of the region had been affected by the war and most of its smaller towns razed. He estimated the number of displaced persons at one million. Addis Ababa radio reported heavy loss of life and put the cost of the war at 1,000 million birr or $479 million.

* The ELF-PLF with its clear understanding of the Ethiopian Dergue's behaviour over Eritrea was not involved in this affair.

36. A massive exodus began in 1977 which has been going on ever since. The war conditions which impelled people to leave and cross into Somalia and Kenya in 1977-78 have been superseded by the consequences of unremitting resistance on the part of the WSLF and the Oromo Liberation Front (OLF) to central government authority. Particularly unsettling to the Oromo and Somali peoples of Hararghe, Bale and Sidamo would appear to be measures to suppress their distinct linguistic and cultural patterns, the drafting of men into the People's Militia and the government's relocation programme. Within this programme, now implemented with some international assistance, substantial numbers of people from central parts of the country, notably Wollo administrative region (repeatedly affected by drought) are being transferred to lands the Oromos and Somalis traditionally considered theirs. Centuries which have inculcated a built-in resistance to change are proving difficult to counteract. The Government strenuously attempts to identify those sympathizing with the liberation movements in order to eliminate all opposition to official policies.

37. Another guerrilla group opposing the central Government is the Tigre People's Liberation Front (TPLF), which in 1978 suffered two major reverses but has since recovered and has continued to operate. Peoples of the northern province of Tigre, already impoverished by adverse conditions of the past including the famine of 10 years ago, have been buffeted about by the military activities of the opposing forces, many driven towards the Sudan border which not a few have crossed to find refuge from the ongoing violence.

38. Over and above these impediments to peace and social progress, the onslaught of drought conditions has affected much of the country. The economy, adversely affected *inter alia* by the dislocations of war and of internal conflict, has a GNP of no more than about $130 per capita (1979 figure).

39. At the same time, violations of human rights other than those implicit in the foregoing paragraphs have been reported by Amnesty International and other groups committed to furthering respect for human rights. Among the alleged violations have been a persecution campaign against the non-orthodox Protestant churches, persecution of the Falasha Jews and the torture and disappearances of political prisoners.

40. The Governments concerned have at various times referred to the causes of uprooting and of flight from Ethiopia. Replying to a communication from the Special Rapporteur, the Government of Ethiopia stated that in its view the Government of Somalia's claim to be sheltering 1.5 million refugees from Ethiopia was 'propaganda' and 'fabrication', suggesting that Somalia had 'changed its war-wounded, orphans and widows into "refugees" . . . to provoke international sympathy and secure food, financial and other assistance.' The letter went on to say:

'The presence of Ethiopians in neighbouring Sudan must be viewed in relation to the war of secession that has been going on in Northern Ethiopia and which has been encouraged, financed and armed by some governments that are bent on creating disharmony in the country and on depriving Ethiopia of its historic outlet to the Red Sea.

'In the same vein, immediately after the eruption of the Ethiopian revolution, counter-revolutionary forces bent on restoring the discredited and crumbling old order, made numerous attempts to create havoc and destruction in Ethiopia. In the effort to counter these forces of evil, innocent people have been forced to flee and seek sanctuary in Sudan and Djibouti.'

41. Writing to the Special Rapporteur, the Government of Sudan said:

'The causes of the influx of these refugees are attributable to the existence of a cultural diversity and religious, social and ethnic differences between the region of Eritrea and the rest of Ethiopia. These differences led the majority of Eritreans to reject Ethiopian rule and demand independence. Large numbers of Eritreans joined liberation movements and a civil war broke out between them and the Ethiopian Government forces. The failure to establish any form of negotiation or dialogue between the two sides aggravated the problem and prolonged the state of war. The consequent lack of security and stability led to a continued influx of Eritrean refugees into the Sudan.'

42. The numbers of those affected by all these events cannot be ascertained with absolute accuracy. However, since 1980 the Government of Ethiopia has spoken of 2.4 million internally displaced, while the Governments of Djibouti, Somalia and the Sudan have put at 45,000, 1.5 million and well over 400,000 respectively the numbers of people who have sought asylum on their territories.

43. Djibouti from the time of its independence in 1977 has been severely taxed with the presence of an increasing number of refugees from Ethiopia. The Government has indeed stated tht the 45,000 refugees, many of whom are of urban background, represent no less than 15 per cent of its population and constitute an intolerable burden at a time when the whole Horn of Africa has been suffering from drought conditions. From the beginning, UNHCR, which in 1978 made an appeal for funds for a programme of humanitarian assistance in the Horn, has, in conjunction with WFP, done what it can to provide relief and promote durable solutions. In the absence of work opportunities even for many nationals, however, third country resettlement has so far proved the only viable means of providing a future for people in this group, and even then numbers are so limited that the majority cannot be catered for in this way. An inter-agency mission which visited Djibouti in June 1980 concluded that international assistance under the most favourable terms was an absolute necessity to help the country face its immediate needs as well as its long-term development requirements.

44. The Sudan has reported the first massive influx of refugees of Eritrean origin as occurring in March 1967, when within a few weeks some 26,000 refugees crossed the border, many of them women and children. Further major influxes

occurred in 1970, 1972 and 1975. With intensified military action in Eritrea and Tigre in 1978, many tens of thousands more poured into the Sudan. The Government established as early as 1968 an Office of the Commissioner for Refugees which has worked in close co-operation with all those concerned with what became in the 1970s a complex programme of relief and rural relocation. Several rural settlements were planned from 1968 onwards, but after a number of years the continued waves of arrivals defeated the joint efforts to bring about durable solutions – all the more as a high proportion of those arriving from Eritrea have been urban refugees not eager to integrate in rural areas. Their presence in Khartoum and other cities however was posed some insurmountable problems, since few work opportunities have existed for them and they could not live without assistance.

45. In general, the nearly half million refugees with whom the Sudan has been confronted have affected negatively some provincial educational and medical services which were already fully stretched to provide a minimal service to the local populations. The problems were sufficiently acute for the Government to decide to convene at Khartoum in June 1980 an international conference on the refugee problem and to request the Secretary-General of the United Nations to send an inter-agency mission to assess the needs of the refugees. The mission, which visited the Sudan in 1980, concluded *inter alia* that:

'The serious economic constraints, together with the Government's heavy external debt, make it difficult for the Government to provide normal social services to its own population, much less extend additional services to a large number of refugees. The refugee burden in the eastern province is particularly onerous.

. . . While UNHCR and WFP have been active in supplementing the Government's efforts to assist the refugees and to seek, to a certain extent, more durable solutions, a substantial portion of the needs of the refugees, especially of those spontaneously settled in rural and urban areas, remains uncovered. There is, therefore, a need for more far-reaching and long-term solutions involving development-oriented programmes.' (Document A/35/410)

The mission saw a pressing need to strengthen infrastructure and services in education, training, health and agriculture. Urgent humanitarian and development assistance together with 'pre-implementation sectoral planning assistance' were quantified at almost $230 million. It noted 'a disturbing trend of growing resentment by the tax-paying Sudanese public towards the refugee population', which was in contrast to the hospitable impulses of the early years, when the strains had not yet been felt. It reported that the humanitarian efforts undertaken by the Government of the Sudan contributed to stability in the region and deserved to be amply supported by the international community.

46. The problems in Somalia have been no less dramatic. If the number of border-crossers is still open to interpretation, there is no doubt that a very large

mass of people has arrived from the Ogaden exhibiting various degrees of exhaustion and distress. These Oromos and Somalis for the most part have required assistance which has been provided by the Government of Somalia, by several agencies of the United Nations system, notably UNHCR and WFP and by a host of voluntary organizations, including the League of Red Cross Societies and the Somali Red Cross. By 11 September 1979, numbers of new arrivals were so great and supply problems so serious that the Government in Mogadishu declared a state of emergency and made a further appeal for international help, whereupon the UN Secretary-General arranged for an inter-agency mission to visit the country to identify urgent needs and recommend a comprehensive programme of assistance. The mission, which took place in December 1979, was followed by a second thirteen months later when the level of need was found to have doubled. Requirements estimated at some $235 million were identified, mainly for relief. It was noted that there was a long-term danger of environmental degradation in the rural areas as a result of the heavy concentration of refugees and livestock near available water points. The Government estimated by early 1981 that about three million head of under-nourished cattle had entered the country suffering from diseases not so far prevalent, posing a threat to the national herd already weakened by the prolonged drought.

47. The Government of Somalia, represented at the ICARA Conference* in Geneva in April 1981 by the Minister of Local Government and Rural Development, made it known on that occasion that the country's GNP had fallen from $120 to $90 per capita since the beginning of the refugee influx (which its states represents 20-25 per cent of the total population). The country's development budget had had to be waived because of the priority given to the more pressing problems.

48. The international community has provided considerable relief assistance to refugees from Ethiopia in the countries of asylum. UNHCR, UNICEF, WFP/FAO and WHO quantify their inputs to the end of 1981 at over $200 million. Indeed the Government of Ethiopia has on more than one occasion suggested that the assistance being given in one area while being denied to areas adjacent to it had contributed to the influx of refugees. For its part, it declared a general amnesty and reports steps to assist the 151,000 people it states have already returned as well as the internally displaced. Calling on the international community for substantial assistance, its Relief and Rehabilitation Commission submitted to the inter-agency mission led by the Co-ordinator of UNDRO in July 1980 projects for relief, rehabilitation, manpower development and sectoral development related to the uprooted and returnees which amounted to hundreds of millions of dollars.

49. With regard to the future, the Commissioner for Relief and Rehabilitation of Socialist Ethiopia, Mr Shimelis Adugna, said at the ICARA Conference:

* International Conference on Assistance to Refugees in Africa, April, 1981.

'The refugees from independent Africa, no doubt, need and deserve generous assistance from the international community. But the long-term solution lies fundamentally and to a large measure with the African countries themselves and on the necessary internal and external measures they take either for the removal of the problem itself, or for scaling it down to manageable proportions.'

The Commissioner went on to say that 'humane efforts should go beyond the provisions of relief assistance and should strive to create favourable conditions that would help attack the problem on a long-term basis'. He referred to the view of the OAU Council of Ministers expressed at its 36th Ordinary Session that 'the problem of refugees in Africa can neither be solved on an *ad hoc* basis, nor on perpetual charity handouts, but rather on working out concrete programmes of action that should provide long-term solutions of a permanent nature'.

50. On the same occasion, Somalia's Minister of Local Government and Rural Development. HE Jama Mohamed Ghalib, said in his speech:

'Today, short and long-term assistance is vital, as is the development of an overall strategy aimed at the resolution of the chronic refugee crisis, which so greatly hampers the development of some of the least-developed nations of Africa.

In this context my Government endorses the recent decision of the General Assembly of the United Nations to table an item entitled "International Co-operation to avert new flows of refugees" on its agenda. This step must involve the impartial examination of the root causes of those phenomena. An environment must be created in which these people will return to their homes with a sense of honor and a feeling of security. The international community has a moral responsibility to assist in creating a peaceful atmosphere in which the long-term solution of voluntary repatriation will take place.'

Appendix 2

STATEMENT MADE BY H.E. AMBASSADOR AHMED MOHAMED ADAN
PERMANENT REPRESENTATIVE OF SOMALIA TO THE UNITED
NATIONS AT THE THIRD COMMITTEE ON ASSISTANCE TO REFUGEES.

6 DECEMBER 1982

ASSISTANCE TO REFUGEES IN SOMALIA

Mr Chairman,

I wish to address myself first of all to specific matters arising from the Secretary-General's Report on Assistance to refugees in Somalia (Document A/37/419) and to deal later with larger questions underlying the problem of refugees in the Horn of Africa.

Document A/37/419 contains a very good summary description of the refugee situation in my country and my delegation trusts that member states will approve its recommendations and respond generously to the continuing need for assistance to the refugees in Somalia. A more comprehensive review and in-depth assessment of the situation is given in the Secretary-General's Report on the Inter-Agency Mission which visited Somalia earlier this year at the request of the General Assembly. This Report, contained in Document E/198/40 of 19 March 1982, has not been circulated as a document of the General Assembly, perhaps due to an oversight, but I will refer to some of the larger issues it raises in the course of the comments I wish to make to further clarify or emphasize the information given in the Report before us.

In the first place I wish to stress the point that there are two components to the refugee situation in Somalia. One component is the refugee population living in the camps established for their shelter and the other component is the refugee population in the country at large eking out an existence in the towns, rural centres or border areas.

The thirty five refugee camps in four areas of the country are now well organized to provide the basic needs of shelter, food, water and medicine, thanks to the generous support offered by individual donor countries, by United Nations Agencies and by non-governmental and other organizations. Let me say here that my Government accepts for purposes of planning international assistance the figure of 700,000 registered camp refugees mentioned in the Report. This figure was ascertained as a result of a joint effort by my Government, the Office of the High Commissioner for Refugees, other United Nations agencies operating in Somalia, non governmental organizations working at close hand with the refugees and representatives of donor countries. We are gratified that this firm basis for aid programmes has been established.

Also a matter of great satisfaction to my Government is the arrangement whereby CARE, an independent, non-governmental organization has been given the management of the logistics of food storage, delivery and distribution, relieving the Somali Government of financial and bureaucratic responsibilities beyond its resources.

The co-ordination and delivery to Somali ports of food assistance by the World Food Programme is another area of aid to the refugees in Somalia for which we are deeply grateful. The developments I have just mentioned illustrate the magnificent response of the international community to my Government's request that it assume the largest share of the responsibility of providing for the refugees in the camps.

I must emphasize, however, that the second component of the refugee problem in Somalia, namely the existence of at least 600,000 more refugees in the community at large is an even greater drain on our resources than the camps which, as I have indicated, are supported in large part by external aid. The livelihood of the refugees outside the camps depends on the generosity of relatives or of the population in general, but the over-all effect of their presence is best expressed in the Report of the Inter-Agency Mission which concluded, quote, 'the Somali socio-economic infrastructure is not capable of sustaining this heavy burden' unquote.

Unfortunately, the need for international assistance to sustain the refugees in the camps and to help Somalia cope with the burden on its socio-economic infrastructure has not lessened, although as I have already stated the situation has somewhat been stabilized. The refugees undoubtedly wish to return home under appropriate conditions, and this wish is strongly supported by my Government. We believe that an organized programme of voluntary repatriation would certainly be the best solution to their plight. However, since the refugees have no evidence that conditions have been created for their safe return with guarantees of basic human rights, they have shown no desire to return home and the need for large scale humanitarian assistance remains unchanged.

Certainly, assistance for basic requirements needs to be maintained, at the very least, at the present level, but since the refugees are likely to remain in Somalia for some time, additional support needs to be given now to self-help activities and to services such as education which would enable them to lead dignified and productive lives and achieve a measure of hope for the future.

My Government's concern for this area of refugee support is illustrated by its commitment to provide, with international assistance, schooling for 30,000 refugee children each year for the next four years. The estimated cost is almost 64 million dollars, although the education offered will be of the most rudimentary kind. When one takes into account the fact that there are more than 300,000 children in the camps the extent of the need in one area alone can be seen. While we recognize the necessity of strengthening government services and facilities and of accelerating development projects in refugee areas we cannot do this without increased international support.

In this context, my Government endorses in principle the recommendation contained in the Report before us that refugee programmes should be closely associated with national development schemes and that there should be increasing involvement of Government Ministries in the implementation of refugee projects. Indeed, within the scope of our limited resources we have already begun to do this in such areas as health, education and employment in agriculture and other fields. However, Somalia could not support a greater shift of the refugee burden from the international community to its Government and people. As it is, the Somali people have borne with remarkable fortitude the serious deprivations in all areas of life which have resulted from the refugee situation. We cannot make even more acute the conflict between the legitimate needs of our citizens and those of the refugees. In this situation we appeal once again to the generosity of the international community as we attempt to provide more than mere sustenance to the refugees and to consider their needs in the longer term.

Let me reiterate that my Government agrees that the conclusions and recommendations contained in document A/37/419 are valid and that insofar as they relate to specific action on the part of Somalia we will do everything possible to implement the recommendations.

No praise can be too high for the generosity and support offered by individual member states of this organization, by various United Nations bodies – particularly the Office of the High Commissioner for Refugees which is the co-ordinating body – by international governmental organizations and by the numerous non-governmental organizations working with great dedication to alleviate the plight of the refugees. I take this opportunity to express to them all the gratitude of my Government.

Mr. Chairman, the larger question underlying international efforts to assist the refugees in Somalia and other countries of the Horn of Africa is the achievement of fundamental and durable solutions to the refugee problems of the area. Both the Report before us and the Report of the Inter-Agency Mission emphasize that repatriation is the most appropriate solution. Unfortunately, the forces of oppression and persecution which set in motion the refugee flight into Somalia and other neighbouring countries are still operative, and these forces work against the return of the refugees to their homes.

The bombing of villages, the massacre of nomads, the poisoning of wells, the killing of livestock and even the strafing of refugees from the air as they make their way to border areas – these atrocities have all been reported by the international news media. The genocidal attempt to depopulate Western Somalia and resettle there people from other areas deepens the tragedy of the refugees and sharpens the political problems of our region.

The situation in Western Somalia is succinctly described in one of the case histories appended to the Study of Human Rights and Massive Exoduses prepared by the Special Rapporteur Sadruddin Aga Khan for the Commission on Human Rights,

The case history on Ethiopia states, and I quote 'Particularly unsettling to the Oromo and Somali peoples of Harahghe, Bale and Sidamo would appear to be measures to suppress their distinct linguistic and cultural patterns, the drafting of men into the People's militia and the government's relocation programme. Within this programme, now implemented with some international assistance, substantial numbers of people from central parts of the country, notably Wollo administrative region are being transferred to lands the Oromos and Somalis traditionally considered theirs. . . . The Government strenuously attempts to identify those sympathizing with the liberation movements in order to eliminate all opposition to official policies.'

Commenting on the same situation the German Magazine *Der Spiegel*, in its issue of 16 June 1980 stated that 'Ethiopia's governing Military Council was attempting to solve minority problems with a massive resettlement programme. Provinces not inhabited by the Amhara were rapidly being colonized with farmers from the central province of Shoa.' In contrast, the magazine continued, 'the Ogaden region in which primarily Somalis lives was being systematically depopulated.'

Describing the 'scorched earth' policy which continues to ensure suffering, alienation, death or exile for vast numbers of people, *Der Spiegel* stated, and I quote, 'Ethiopian and Cuban troops go from village to village burning down the huts, poisoning wells and watering holes and shooting down the livestock with machine guns. What the Amhara and Cubans leave falls victim to the drought.'

In its issue of 17 March 1980, *Der Spiegel* describes the political reasons for these cruel policies. 'The tribal transfer', it explained, 'is supposed to help break resistance in the long run. No less than three million people are to be resettled. . . . For the benefit of the outside world Mengistu has masked the action as a humanitarian one. . . . Using the generally favourable cover of resettlement the Government has succeeded in getting the United Nations and the European Community to subsidize the paramilitary operation.'

Comments from impartial sources such as the ones I have quoted bear out the widely acknowleged fact of Ethiopia's infamous relocation programme. In the light of this development, it is necessary for member states to take a close look at the current resolution on Assistance to displaced persons in Ethiopia, contained in document A/C.3/37/L.55, which refers repeatedly to displaced persons and to so-called voluntary returnees in Ethiopia.

A closer look at the polite but sceptical Report of visiting officials of the League of Red Cross Societies who through an agreement signed in Geneva on 29/6/82 had been established as the operational partner of UNHCR, reveal the unsatisfactory nature of their visits to the so-called camps or transit centres for voluntary returnees.

To give but a few short examples, officials of the League who had visited the Red Sea Eritrean port of Massawa on 17/9/82 reported: ' . . . the visit to Massawa was too short to allow of our going to the Dahlac Archipelago where the returnee fishermen are reported to be . . . ' Could their non-visit have been connected with the Soviet naval base which reportedly exists there and would naturally be out of bounds to any such visits? Or to the fact that returnees were non-existent.

During the League officials' visit to the town of Karen in Eritrea they reported finding a well constructed transit camp accommodating 450 people at the time of their visit. They were also told by the Ethiopians that 4000 returnees had already passed through the camp according to the records of the person in charge of the camp. It is significant, however, that the League visitors did not see or talk to the people concerned to establish their identity as voluntary returnees.

Visiting yet another so called transit camp for voluntary returnees in Tessenei in Eritrea, the League officials reported that they had been told by their hosts that the centre accommodated 1,300 people at the time of their visit and that 3,000 more were at other centres in the same area. The League officials stated in their Report, I quote, 'We are not able to establish . . . how many people had been accommodated in Tessenei altogether and no records were in evidence.'

Commenting on yet another visit, this time to Sheikh Sharif Shelter near Jigjiga in the Ogaden, the League officials stated and I quote, 'There was no registration of inhabitants of the shelter, but it was thought that 11,000 had left for their former homes.' There were told that at the time of their visit there were approximately 5,000 people living in the shelter. The Report continued to state that, and I quote, 'people were not interviewed because weather conditions dictated a rapid departure of their Ethiopian supplied DC3 aircraft' – a strange coincidence indeed!

I could go on quoting from the Report of the officials of the League, but I not wish to take up the time of the Committee with more of the same. But our insistence for the devising of a foolproof system through which any voluntary returnees could be monitored and their credentials established will be appreciated in the light of the deliberately casual manner in which things are now being done in the matter of voluntary returnees as revealed by the Report of the League of Red Cross Societies.

The UNHCR Report concerning the launching of a programme of $20 million for the settlement of 15,000 returnees, has already been overtaken by the figure of 150,000 given by the Ethiopian Commissioner for Relief and Rehabilitation in this speech before this Committee in November. It is clear that the Commissioner increased the number by simply adding one more zero to the High Commissioner's figure! If we are not careful, the same device could be used again next year, to confront the international community with a figure of 1.500.000 of so-called voluntary returnees in the same manner that the international community is being called upon to assist 5 million drought-stricken and 2.4 million displaced persons – numbers which must be treated with scepticism since they have not been ascertained beyond reasonable doubt.

Significantly, the Representative of the Sudan recently stated before this Committee that the influx of refugees into the Sudan continued unabated.

With regard to Somalia, the continuing massive presence of refugees there, and the surveys carried out among them by international groups indicate that refugees are not returning home from Somalia. From where, then may we ask, are these returnees coming?

A further, and I may say a typical discrepancy in Ethiopian claims, lies in the fact that until very recently they have maintained that the refugees in Somalia were not from Ethiopia but were destitute Somali citizens. Today Ethiopia is asking for international assistance to resettle returnees from Somalia whose existence they have persistently denied. Obviously Ethiopia cannot have it both ways.

My delegation believes it is important to direct the attention of member states to the need to determine with reasonable accuracy the numbers and true origin of so-called displaced persons and returnees in Ethiopia. The necessary assessments cannot be made on the basis, for example, of hurried visits under close Ethiopian supervision to rural areas by representatives of the League of Red Cross Societies, however well intentioned such visits may have been.

Ethiopia, which has repeatedly accused Somalia in the past of inflating refugee figures has not opened its refugee operations to the kind of impartial, extensive and widely based international scrutiny which has established the number of refugees in the camps of Somalia. Instead it has resisted all but the most cursory examinations of its claims. Until it is prepared to change its attitude, the figures given of 2.4 million displaced persons, 150,000 returnees, and 5 million drought-stricken people must remain in question, particularly so because of the grave suspicion that many of these people are merely Ethiopians which are being relocated for political purposes.

The ability of the Ethiopian Government to use humanitarian assistance for sinister ends was pointed out by the Somali delegation two years ago in the debate on the same items before us now. We expressed then our deep concern over the request for 11 million dollars for the upgrading of the airstrip at Gode in occupied Ogaden, ostensibly so that relief aid could be freighted there for distribution to camps for displaced and drought-stricken people in the Ogaden. The airstrip at Gode, improved through international assistance, has been used this year as a base for the large-scale and sustained military aggressions launched by land and air against my country. The concern we expressed two years ago was indeed justified.

Mr. Chairman, it seems clear to my delegation that member states must address themselves to a number of issues pertaining to the refugee situation in the Horn of Africa and the response of the international community to that situation. First, there must be more rigorous international supervision of the use of humanitarian assistance. Somalia has been falsely and scurrilously accused by Ethiopia of mismanagement and misappropriation of aid. We suggest that Ethiopia which is itself open to grave charges of the misuse of humanitarian assistance should follow the example we have set in turning over the management of aid to an impartial agency. Secondly, there must be a closer monitoring of the numbers and the nature of so-called displaced persons.

Inflated figures by the Ethiopian authorities must not be accepted at their face value. Third, in the context of assessing the need for humanitarian assistance for returnees, a system should be established for the monitoring of voluntary returnees at agreed, specific check points so that their credentials as genuine returnees can be ascertained.

As my delegation said in November 1980, let all refugees be protected and sustained; let genuinely displaced persons be fed, assisted and resettled. But let us not in the process stoke the very fires that are the basic cause of their plight.

While making every effort to extend humanitarian assistance to those who are genuinely deprived, we must exert the greatest care to ensure that we do not unwittingly support unjust, aggressive and even genocidal policies. Only when such policies are ended can there be hope for a peaceful, just, humane and durable solution to the refugee problem in the Horn of Africa.

Appendix 3

RIGHT OF REPLY
BY AMBASSADOR AHMED MOHAMED ADAN
BEFORE THE THIRD COMMITTEE
7 DECEMBER, 1982

Mr Chairman,

Just before we adjourned our meeting yesterday afternoon, the committee was subjected to an emotional outburst by the representative of Ethiopia, ostensibly in the exercise of his right of reply to a statement which I had made earlier in the day on the question of assistance to the refugees in Somalia. When he had concluded his agitated vituperations, I asked for the floor in order to tell you that I had no desire to dignify his despicable comments with a reply. However, since I could not have the floor then for technical reasons, I had time to reflect on the matter as a result of which I feel duty bound to set the record straight.

The Ethiopian representative began his intervention by attacking me personally. He also arrogated to himself the right of speaking on your behalf by stating that I had not heeded your appeal to me following his impertinent and repeated interruption of my statement. Similarly he transformed himself into a self-styled spokesman for the other members of the committee when he accused me of throwing dust in their eyes. Those matters, I think, should have been left for you and for the member of the committee to judge for themselves.

His disparaging remarks that I was an occasional visitor to this committee who was not in tune with the cooperative spirit of its deliberations were also irrelevant and uncalled for. You, Mr. Chairman, and other members of the Committee, are aware that I am represented on this committee by my deputy who keeps me well informed of what goes on here. In fact, it is the Ethiopian representative who is an occasional visitor to these United Nations – I think he comes once a year – and who is out of touch with the realities of the work of this Organization. His briefs and instructions which he brings from his capital are often times out of step with those realities.

The Ethiopian representative in his intervention attempted to capitalize on the preference of members of this committee and of yourself, Mr. Chairman, to keep humanitarian issues polemic-free, when he knows fully well that it is his delegation which continually violates the need for restraint on this matter, even to the extent of breaking prior agreements reached through the good offices of some African members. To cite the most recent example, the item before us was last considered in New York by the Economic and Social Council at its first regular session in 1982. It was then agreed by the Somali and the Ethiopian delegations that both should refrain from injecting polemics into the debate to enable the committee to adopt the relevant resolutions by consensus, and to promote a spirit of cooperation between the two delegation, at least on those issues which are humanitarian in nature. Distinguished delegates will remember that no sooner had the ECOSOC adopted the resolutions than the Ethiopian representative took out from his brief case a well prepared statement, attacking Somalia in the kind of abusive language which it has become the habit of Ethiopian representatives to employ in their interventions against my country. In the light of Ethiopia's consistent use of the refugee issue as a means of attacking Somalia in this and other fora, how could its representative allow himself to shed crocodile tears in regard to the need for moderation in debating humanitarian issues? Why the double standards?

Mr. Chairman, it is not my intention to stoop to the level to which the Ethiopian Representative lowered himself in his intervention yesterday, nor is it my desire to return in kind his attack against my person.

There is, however, one thing which bothers me. Whenever the Ethiopian representative has occasion to comment on Somalia – be it on humanitarian or other issues – he consistently decends to the level of attacking the Somali head of state in person and by name. I often often wonder what forces impel him to do so, for I am sure that to make unwholesome remarks against heads of state, particularly before U.N. deliberative bodies such as this committee, is to be guilty of bad taste, to say the least. Is it because his instructions prescribe that he should do so? Or could it be that he does it out of his own volition in order to provoke me into retaliating in kind against his own head of state, and if so what are his ulterior motives for provoking such an attack against his head of state? I do not wish to emulate him, but he must know that my patience is not unlimited, and whether his vicious utterances against my President is in compliance with his instructions, or are of his own choice for reasons best known to himself, he cannot expect me to be silent on this issue in the future, and we all know of the repression the persecution and the alienation which the Ethiopian people have gone through during the leadership of his current head of state.

The reasons for his angry tirade against my country, My President, and my person is clear, for in my statement yesterday morning I touched a raw nerve in Ethiopia's diabolical plans to depopulate certain regions in order to resettle them with peoples from other regions with the unwitting subsides of the international community. This programme of relocation has been mentioned in the case-study of the Special Rapporteur, I quote 'Within this programme, now implemented with some international assistance, substantial numbers of people from central parts of the country, notably Wollo administrative region (repeatedly affected by drought) are being transferred to lands which the Oromos and Somalis traditionally considered theirs.' In corroboration of this DER SPIEGAL also states 'because the Ethiopian army . . . has not succeeded in uniting by force of arms the disparate nationalities of Ethiopia, the people of

80

that country must now be formed into new groups through depopulation in order to make way for resettlement by new inhabitants . . . Using the generally favourable cover of resettlement, the regime has succeeded in getting the U.N. and the European community to subsidize its para-military operation.' This is why, Mr. Chairman, Somalia is convinced that the so-called voluntary returnees are not returnees at all but are part and parcel of this relocation programme. Ethiopia has consistently denied the existence of refugees in Somalia, a denial which was repeated by its representative in his intervention yesterday and again today. But in the same breath they insist on a programme for voluntary returnees in such areas of the Ogaden which are contiguous with Somalia.

Thus, on the one hand Ethiopia denies the existence of refugees in Somalia at all but on the other hand permits itself to cast aspersions on their numbers. Mr. Chairman in page 4 paragraph 9 of its report in Doc. E/1982/40 of 19/3/82 the U.N. Inter Agency Mission states, I quote: 'After discussions with the government, representatives of donor countries, and international and non-governmental organizations in Somalia, the Mission recommends that the international relief programme for 1982 be planned on the basis of the camp population of 700,000 refugees. . . In addition an estimated 700,000-800,000 refugees, mostly nomads, were dispersed throughout the country or concentrated in urban centres.'

Also the UNHCR in his report in Doc. Supplement No. 12 (A/37/12) states, I quote 'A planning figure of 700,000 people in refugee camps was agreed upon in early 1982 between the United Nations Inter-Agency Mission to Somalia and the Somalia government.' The report continues to state that: 'To improve the delivery and distribution of food, an emergency logistics unit was created and its management entrusted to a voluntary agency.' The facts contained in those reports constitute a fitting answer to the Ethiopian representative's often repeated cheap allegations on the numbers of the refugees in Somalia and the distribution of food aid to them.

In contrast, Ethiopia claims to have 5 million drought-stricken people, 2.4 million displaced persons and now 150,000 returnees, which by the way is ten times the figure of 15,000 in the High Commissioner's report. Added together these figure total more than 7.5 million persons. But so far Ethiopia has resisted any attempt that these figure be checked, as it has resisted the supervision of the proper use of humanitarian aid which is extended by the international community. In the circumstances I should like to close my intervention by repeating the concluding remarks of my statement of yesterday morning. I quote, 'We suggest that Ethiopia which is open to grave charges of the misuses of humanitarian assistance should follow the example we have set in turning over the management of aid to an impartial agency. Secondly, there must be a closer monitoring of the numbers and the nature of so-called displaced persons. Inflated figures by the Ethiopian authorities must not be accepted at their face value. Third, in the context of assessing the need for humanitarian assistance for returnees, a system should be established for the monitoring of voluntary returnees at agreed, specific check points so that their credentials as genuine returnees can be ascertained.

Appendix 4

DELEGATION TO ICARA II
PRESS RELEASE

The Government of the Somali Democratic Republic welcomes and fully supports the Second International Conference on Aid to Refugees in Africa and totally endorses its humanitarian ideals and aims and its timely sponsorship by the United Nations Organization and the Organization of African Unity.

However, the Somali Delegation felt obliged to leave the Conference Hall temporarily this morning in order to register principled protest against the appearance of a representative of the repressive Ethiopian ruling Junta. It is indeed ironic after so inspiring an address by the Secretary General of the United Nations, that a spokesman with such dubious credentials should be so hypocritical as to take the floor and claim to be delivering a statement on the current refugee crisis on behalf of Africa.

It is common knowledge that the cruel policies of repression, terror and genocide practiced by this same regime against the oppressed peoples within the empire-state is the major cause of the massive refugee flows into Somalia and sister African countries of such concern to the world community. These flows together constitute the major element in the refugee tragedy sadly afflicting our beloved continent today.

Geneva
9.7.84

Appendix 5

REFUGEES
PRESS STATEMENT 23 OCTOBER 1984

The Government of the Somali Democratic Republic has observed that a measure of credence appears to have been accorded to un-substantiated and quite false reports emanating from Ethiopia on the subject of so-called 'returnee' refugees.

This is the more surprising in view of the clarity of a recent statement made jointly in Khartoum by the Refugee Commissioners of the Sudan and Somalia. It confirmed that although 'voluntary repatriation remains the most viable solution for the refugees' problem, once the causes of their flight have been removed there had been no refugee – or returnee – flows from the Sudan and Somalia into neighbouring countries.

Mr Hugh Hudson, the UNHCR information department official who accompanied the Deputy High Commissioner on his recent visit to Somalia, has reported that 'continuous movement into the Ogaden region by small numbers of refugees from Somalia takes the form of a nomadic to-and-fro, in a pattern which predates the present refugee crisis by centuries'. These small groups are not of course 'returnees', and there are none others.

Ethiopia's recent claims to the contrary are pure fiction and have not been in any way substantiated or supported either by the UNHCR office in Somalia or by CARE, to whom the Government has entrusted the day-to-day administration and distribution of relief and food supplies, or by any of the many concerned international and voluntary agencies assisting the National Refugee Commission in the enormous humanitarian tasks resulting from the massive flows of refugees who have long sought, and are still seeking, safe sanctuary in the Somali Democratic Republic.

In this context, the Government also deplores the bombing and strafing of Somali towns and settlements by Ethiopian warplanes, which has become an almost daily occurrence, not to mention the continued occupation of sections of Somali territory by Ethiopian military forces.

The Government has the duty to warn the international community that Ethiopian agents have been discovered endeavouring to buy refugee identity and ration cards, presumably to take them to Ethiopia as 'evidence' of non-existent flows of 'returnees'. Moreover, the Ethiopian occupation forces in the Haud, the Ogaden and elsewhere, including Eritrea, have commenced calling local populations to gather at assembly points, supposedly in order to benefit

83

from food distributions but actually to provide apparent 'evidence' of refugee returnee flows which have not in fact occurred.

A glance at the verbatim records of the relevant United Nations fora in Geneva and New York will reveal many instances where Ethiopia's official delegates have sought to deny the very existence of the refugees they now claim are returning in vast numbers. Moreover, the mis-use of food aid to support the many oppressive wars the regime in Addis Ababa is conducting against the Western Somalis, the Eritreans, the Tigreans, the Oromo and Sidama and other peoples is well documented, and should give cause for thought.

The Somali Government stresses that it would be the last to discourage international relief of the people's genuine suffering in any state. But in the strife-stricken Ethiopian empire, most of those who are indeed in great and critical need are to be found in liberated areas, well outside the control or even access of the Addis Ababa regime.

Regrettably, there appears no doubt at all that the Ethiopian Dergue, with a cynical eye on current international humanitarian concern for the victims of famines and other natural and man-made disasters in Africa, is seeking to attract aid that can then be diverted to support the oppressive military activities now being planned as a prelude to the tenth anniversary of the so-called 'revolution' of 1974.

It is to this ignoble end that the Ethiopian regime seeks to intimidate militarily and to subvert politically its neighbours whilst at the same time falsely seeking international acclaim as the supposed 'host' of non-existent flows of 'returnee-refugees'.

Appendix 6

DJIBOUTI: THE TRUTH –
BRIEFING BY A NEWLY-ARRIVED REFUGEE FROM
DJIBOUTI

Composition of the refugee community

Large numbers of refugees started to arrive in Djibouti in 1978 as a result of the fighting between local people in the Ogaden and the major conflict between Somalia and Ethiopia. These were primarily Issas.

Since that time more people have arrived from varying backgrounds and from deeper inside Ethiopia. These have included peasants who have political problems, young people and others who have political affiliations or sympathies. Since 1979 the situation of the Afars inside Ethiopia has deteriorated and many have fled to Djibouti.

The flight from Ethiopia, largely to avoid political and religious persecution, is still going on. During 1983 there were an average of 3 new arrivals in Djibouti every day. This number has now increase and at present it is running at about 8-10 a day. Military service and the recent harrassment of Oromos and some other individuals inside Ethiopia is largely responsible.

Situation on the Ethio-Djibouti border

Refugees arriving across the border are often refused and are sent back. What most refugees try to do is to sneak in and then present themselves at the camp at Ali Sabieh. In many cases those who are not handed over to the Dergue at the border are detained for from 10 days to 2 weeks. The UNHCR are not involved at this stage and do not know what is going on.

Organisation of camps

By and large the refugees are kept in two major camps:
   i. Ali Sabieh, in which there is a transit section, where new arrivals wait for documentation.
   The occupants of Ali Sabieh are mainly Issas and other refugees such as the Oromos, Tigrays etc. who are regarded as 'politicals'.
   ii. The Afars are kept in Dikil camp.
   The UNHCR has its branch office in Dikil. It has been there since all the

advisory services, such as the medical and counselling services, were moved from Djiboutiville. The conditions in the camps have improved since 1979, when all the refugees were housed in tents; some are now in houses. There is also a basic health service and a school for the children. Whilst the conditions are poor, it has to be remembered that the conditions of Djibouti nationals are also very inadequate.

Registration

It takes about a year to get registration as a refugee, if he is in one of the camps. It is not known exactly how many refugees there are in Djibouti, but the figure is certainly significant. For example if you have a friend who is a Djibouti national or have a family member living in Djibouti, it is possible to live under his protection and people in this situation do not even know anything about registration. It is possible, therefore, that there are even more than the 31,000 claimed by the UNHCR. There are also many Somali-speaking people who cross backwards and forwards across the border and have, in effect, dual nationality. In some cases these people are mixed up with refugees.

It is also possible to get registration papers by bribing officials or providing services to them e.g. prostitution.

The UNHCR are on the Eligibility Commission which decides on refugee applications for registration. Their performance is not considered satisfactory by refugees. For example, one refugee, who had been a political prisoner in Ethiopia, escaped to Djibouti after his release. He had with him a paper confirming his prison sentence and that it had been given on political grounds. When he showed this to the UNHCR they told him that they could not support his application. This happened in August, 1983.

Refugees in Djiboutiville

The UNHCR does not offer any protection or services to refugees living outside the camps. In spite of this a number of refugees continue to live in Djiboutiville. There are two main reasons for this:
  i. the camp at Dikil (to which they are sent) is only 5kms from the Ethiopian border
  ii. it is very isolated from the outside world and it is not possible to make contacts with anyone outside the camp. Refugees who are in the camps are *de facto* internees and cannot leave. As all refugees hope to get out of Djibouti eventually, they find this very restrictive.

Life in Djiboutiville is very insecure. Refugees are not allowed to work and now receive no allowances from the UNHCR. Often they live together in one room, and one person in a group may be working illegally, supporting the others as well as himself. Some of the young women are driven to prostitution to support themselves and often they also support others out of sympathy with their predicament. Numbers of others live in Protestant and Catholic churches or in Mosques, depending on charity.

There are no employment prospects in Djibouti, which is without resources and has high unemployment. Many Djiboutians leave the country to work in the Middle East, so there is no incentive to refugees to enter Djibouti in search of a better life. The climate is also extremely harsh.

Roughs

The practice of rounding people up and deporting them in what are known as 'roughs' goes back to French colonial times. The French used roughs as a means of picking up 'illegal immigrants' and returning them to their own countries (largely Somalia) or to pick up suspected dissidents during the struggle for independence during house to house sweeps. The Djibouti government took over this system and have been mounting 'roughs' ever since independence and have extended them to include refugees. In the early 1980s and particularly in 1982 the gendarmerie would search houses regularly and load those they found without I.D. cards on to trucks or trains destined for Ethiopia. In the past year most roughs have taken place in the streets, with the gendarmerie arrested people as they walked along. This now happens frequently and it is difficult for anyone picked up in this way to get help, especially if there happens to be a train going to Diredawa on the day or night of arrest. There have been many cases in which people have jumped out of trucks or committed suicide to avoid being deported to Ethiopia.

During a 'rough' period, all refugees tend to stay indoors and do not venture out until police activity has died down. They then go out again and the whole cycle is repeated.

Repatriation

In spite of the harsh conditions in Djibouti, refugees have always been unwilling to return to Ethiopia. In 1979 the Dergue's Administrator from Hararghe visited Dikil Camp bearing an amnesty for the refugees and promising them compensation for goods and property lost. His overtures were totally rejected. In 1982 the refugees were put under severe pressures to persuade them to leave Djibouti. This carrot and stick operation culminated in the establishment of the Tripartite Commission, consisting of the Ethiopian and Djibouti Governments, together with the UNHCR. The Commission's job was to work out a programme of repatriation.

In February, 1983 the Tripartite Commission announced that its programme was being put together and would be ready in 15 days. Either way, the announcement caused panic amongst the refugees. Many tried to escape. Hundreds walked to Somalia and others went in ships to Kenya and other countries. 20 Oromos went on one ship alone. Some of those who left were stowaways, who landed up at places like Mombasa and Saudi Arabia. One man who stowed away was, unknown to him, on a ship destined for Assab and was arrested by the Ethiopians as soon as the ship docked. Others, who reached Saudi Arabia, claimed that they were Eritreans when they were caught by the Saudis and were sent to the Eritrean coast.

The term 'voluntary' in the Agreement drawn up by the Tripartite Commission is not important. No attempt was made to ask whether people would be willing to return but a budget for repatriating 31,000 was drawn up. All three participants were totally committed to the operation from the beginning. Again the carrot and stick method was used.

Immediately following the finalisation of the programme, gendarmes visited the camps and told people that they would all be repatriated and threatened them if they did not sign on. This was followed by a gradual reduction of the rations in Ali Sabieh Camp and again people were told that there would be no food for those who did not agree to go. On the other hand, a UNHCR-sponsored Refugee Committee were taken to the resettlement areas, where they were given a warm reception by the Ethiopian government. One Oromo woman who went later said that she was not imprssed, but there was no formal meeting with the rest of the refugees at which they could ask questions. Also important was the Ethiopian Government's use of the Issas chief from Ethiopia in their efforts to persuade refugees to return. The chief, Ugaz Hassan, had represented the Issas at Haile Selassie's Imperial Court, and is still influential with the Dergue. He is reported to have told the Issas refugees in Ali Sabieh to accept repatriation as 'it made no difference' to them, meaning that they could go backwards and forwards to Djibouti as they wished, taking tools and handouts back to Djibouti if they wanted to do so.

It was, however, the reduction of rations that had the most serious effect on the refugees.

Those returned to date are predominantly Issas, who are being resettled along the railway line in Ethiopia.

So far the Afars have not been returned en masse, although pressure on them and others in Dikil camp is being stepped up. The UNHCR maintain that the Issas are being returned to an area of peace. Whether or not this is true, they cannot make this claim about the Afars areas. Afars resistance is still continuing and there are a number of other fronts in the Afars area, notably the TPLF which is able to make attacks and raids. Quite recently, the Ethiopian army entered Djibouti in hot pursuit of Afars who had fled following a skirmish and attacked villages inside Djibouti. The refugees at Djibouti had to be restrained from going to their aid, thus demonstrating their continuing hostility to the Ethiopians. If they are to be returned, therefore, they will have to be resettled deeper inside Ethiopia and not in their home areas.

Ethiopian Government support for Repatriation

At a time when the Ethiopian government is asking for massive aid to help famine victims it may seem odd that the Ethiopians should want 30,000-plus refugees back. In fact, they have an interest in the completion of the Djibouti operation. The fact that Ethiopia is presented as a peaceful country to which refugees can safely return enhances the Dergue's prestige in the international community. It has also brought in considerable sums of much-needed money for resettlement projects. At the same time, it could bring in new, easily-conscripted recruits for the Ethiopian army, although there is some evidence that the Dergue is somewhat displeased to find that most of the refugees are women, children and old people, most of the young people having escaped to Somalia and elsewhere.

The Djibouti Government

The Djibouti Government is a signatory to the Convention and its relevant protocols. There is no doubt, however, that the country is ill-equipped to cater for so many refugees. Refugees do not, however, see the Djiboutians as the main force behind the repatriation on these grounds, in spite of UNHCR hints that they are.

Since independence Djibouti has been under considerable pressure from its powerful neighbour, Ethiopia. At the time of independence, dissident Afars fled to Ethiopia and were trained by the Dergue to destabilize Djibouti. Following negotiations between the two Governments in 1981/2 the weaker elements of this group were secretly returned to Djibouti, but the hard core remain inside Ethiopia, where they continue to threaten the government there. The Djibouti Government knows that the Dergue would not hesitate to use them if necessary.

At the same time, Ethiopia is Djibouti's main source of revenue vis-a-vis the port, as 80% of the goods imported go to Ethiopia.

These pressures from Ethiopia are irresistable. The Ethiopians have, for instance, demanded the return of some 'political' refugees, who have been refouled and taken to Addis Ababa where they are charged with having left the country illegally. Prison sentences for this offence range from 1 to 15 years. On one occasion the Ethiopian Radio referred to one group of such political refugees who had been returned and imprisoned 'with the co-operation of the Djibouti authorities'.

In December, 1983, groups of refugees in Ali Sabieh were also screened for political involvement and their details passed on to the Ethiopian authorities.

Not all refugees who have been refouled have been imprisoned; some have been sent straight to the battlefronts according to information received in Djibouti.

Refugees and the UNHCR

Relations between the refugees have always been poor. Today they are almost non-existent. The Ethiopian Refugee Committee which was established in the latter 70s and made representations on behalf of all the refugees is now banned. The Oromo Refugee Association of Djibouti, which has acted on behalf of the Oromo refugees on many occasions and used to help the UNHCR is now also in disfavour. The recent case of an Oromo who was picked up in Djiboutiville and who jumped from a truck and was killed has led to ORAD being regarded with deep suspicion by UNHCR. This is because there was publicity about the case outside Djibouti. The UNHCR went so far as to send staff to the house from which the funeral was being arranged. Later police demanded the names of ORAD member, and even arrested a Djibouti national in the house because he could not give names. Other Oromos who have been to UNHCR are asked the same questions and ORAD believe that the UNHCR are carrying on a witch-hunt against them.

At an individual level refugees have no faith in UNHCR, who do not seem to be able to protect them and appear to have close connections with Djibouti security. Refugees also believe that if the UNHCR had stood up to the Djibouti Government over *refoulement* and the repatriation issue, that government would have responded as the Djiboutians do not have any ill-will towards the refugees. More international aid could have helped considerable to relieve the accepted pressures, for example, on the Djibouti economy.

Some UNHCR personnel who have seemed hesitant about their role have changed their attitudes dramatically after they have made routine visits to Ethiopia; no-one knows what happens there. Most of the UNHCR staff, like those of other agencies, seem, however, to be specially selected for Djibouti. By and large they are only interested in their own careers and are not therefore willing to say anything about what is going on in Djibouti.

The UNHCR also keep visitors, and particularly journalists, away from the refugees, and especially those who are in Djiboutiville, who could give a good account of refugee affairs. In recent months, UNHCR officials have refused to see refugees themselves.

The fate of returnees

It is not possible for the UNHCR or anyone else to monitor the fate of returnees beyond the point at which they are handed over from the trains to the various local authorities in Ethiopia. It is known that Ethiopian security are represented on the reception committees.

When, at the end of 1983, a train from Djibouti to Diredawa was blown up, probably by the Western Somali Liberation Front, many refugees were fearful of suffering the same fate if they returned, their feelings were ignored and repatriation is still going on. This is indicative of the determination of the Tripartite Commission to push through the total repatriation of the refugees.

The refugees most at risk are those who do not have connections with the groups in Djibouti. There are both Issas and Afars members of the Djibouti Government and in some cases, if the right people are approached, either they or the relevant groups amongst the gendarmerie can get a reprieve for refugees who are being sent to Ethiopia. This is not possible for others, such as the Oromos and Tigrayans, who have no-one to turn to. Their only hope to is get a female family member or friend married to a Djiboutian, who will then protect her and those who are connected with her. Rather than return to Ethiopia young women are quite prepared to enter into such a marriage.

14 August, 1984

Appendix 7

"IMPLEMENTING A POLICY DECISION"
COPY OF A DOCUMENT SMUGGLED OUT OF ETHIOPIA

(I) ATTESTATION

I, Abreha Hailemikael, do swear that the attached photocopy bearing my signature is a copy of the original document, a letter delivered to me by the Representative, for Wollega Province, Ethiopia, of the Archives Section (Dept) of the Relief and Rehabilitation Commission on February 26, 1983 (Yekatit 18, 1975 Ethiopian calendar).

I, Abreha Hailemikael, further state that I served as the Regional Representative for Wollega of the Relief and Rehabilitation Commission of the Ethiopian Government, in which capacity I received the attached letter (copy), until October 4, 1983.

The attached document (copy) was carried by me out of Ethiopia in October, 1983.

Signed,

Abreha Hailemikael

(II) DOCUMENT

18, Yekatit, 1975 E.C.
(25 February, 1983)

Re: Implementing a Policy Decision

The Property and Transport Services Council
The Finance Services Council
RRC
Addis Ababa

You would recall that the Commission had earlier received a consignment of 15,717 tons of wheat, 629 tons of milk and 629 tons of oil donated by the UN World Food Programme to feed an estimated 85,900 settlers in Asosa, Harewa and Anger-Gutin.

However, of the food aid that was given:

1st   12524 tons of wheat was given in exchange to ISGED (the Amharic abbreviation for the Agricultural Crops Marketing Corporation) at the Port. Furthermore, the office of the Relief Commission delivered 3193 tons by mistake to the Ministry of Agriculture which has not been returned to the Commission so far.

2nd The Commission received a consignment of 1258 tons of milk and oil. It distributed part of it in the settlement projects, part for relief work elsewhere, and the balance is still in our store.

Although the agreement for the food aid stipulates that it is to be used solely in aid of the three emergency settlement projects, the Commission used part of the available aid for relief in other provinces that had crop and food shortages. This was not communicated to the donors at the time.

We are aware that having failed to act in accordance with the agreement the chances for the country getting further food aid could be adversely affected.

The matter is the more worrying now that an auditor is here with us in Ethiopia today, 17 Yekatit 1975 (24 February 1983) to assess how the food aid for these projects has been distributed and used.

The food aid has not been strictly used for the intended projects in accordance with the agreement. However, in order to provide the auditor with the necessary evidence when he is out surveying, we have decided that you should act according to the policy decisions outlined below:

1st   *Regarding the 1258 tons of milk and oil intended for the three projects.*
You are to record in your record books the exact amount of oil and milk intended for each project area as if it has actually been issued in full from the RRC warehouse at Awash and despatched. You are to make available the books to the auditor for his inspection.

2nd   *Regarding the maize which should have been received from ISGED in exchange.*
The Commission had reported to the donors that it had received a certain quantity of maize from ISGED in exchange for the wheat it had delivered to them. You are therefore to record in your books that the said quantity had been issued from the RRC warehouse in Addis Ababa and Nazareth and to make the books available for the auditor.

3rd   The 3193 metric tons of wheat which the Commission is owed by the Ministry of Agriculture will have to be repaid by the Ministry of Agriculture at a later date. You are nevertheless to report to the Organisation that it has already been repaid and already utilized as intended.

4th   Regarding documentation for the expenditure of the money received from the donors to cover Port and local transport expenses you are to assume that all the payment has been made to the Maritime and Transit Services Corporation. The Corporation will send the proforma invoice it had specifically prepared for the purpose through the Financial Services Council who will sign and pass on to the office of the Organisation in Addis Ababa.

5th   When the auditor arrives at Asosa to review the general progress of the work you will have ready for inspection in your office records showing that all the food aid planned for the project has been actually received and duly recorded in your books.

6th   To fulfill the conditions listed from 1-6, a carefully selected three-man committee led by a representative of the Audit and Inspection Service Council, together with representatives from the Financial Services Council and Administrative Services Council shall be formed. In order to prepare the necessary vouchers, the committee shall be given new unused vouchers from the Property and Transport Council and shall post in the books for each project area the exact amount of aid received and distributed. They will do so in accordance with the directives that shall be issued by the Council.

7th   You are hereby instructed to collect all the documents used by the auditor as soon as he completes his inspection and mark them VOID and present a report. Regarding the handling of the duplicate copies in the receipt books you shall receive further policy guidelines in the future.

Ethiopia First (Tikdem)
End to Hunger

Shimelis Adugna
Chief of Commission

cc Acting Vice Commissioner
Vice Commissioner
Audit and Inspection Service
RRC
Addis Ababa
Officer in charge,
RRC Office Wollega
RRC, wherever he may be

Appendix 8

RESOLUTION OF THE EUROPEAN PARLIAMENT
ON THE HORN OF AFRICA

(A copy of pages 71-78 of the Minutes of Proceedings of the Sitting of Thursday, 12 April 1984. These pages contain the resolution on the Horn of Africa as adopted by the Parliament.)

The European Parliament

— *having regard* to its resolution of 10 May 1979 on respect for human rights in Ethiopia[1],
— *having regard* to its resolution of 14 December 1979 on the tragic plight of refugees, particularly children, in the Horn of Africa[2],
— *having regard* to its resolution of 23 May 1980 on the wretched situation of the refugees in Somalia[3],
— *having regard* to its resolution of 11 July 1980 on the dramatic situation of the refugees, especially the children amongst them, in the Horn of Africa[4],
— *having regard* to its resolution of 18 November 1982 on the situation in Somalia[5],
— *having regard* to its resolution of 14 April 1983 on emergency aid for Ethiopia[6],
— *having regard* to the motion for a resolution tabled by Mr PEDINI and others on behalf of the EPP Group on the situation in the region of Eritrea (Doc. 1-1129/82),
— *having regard* to the motion for a resolution tabled by Mr HAHN and others on the forcible repatriation of Ethiopian refugees in Djibouti (Doc. 1-23/83),
— *having regard* to the resolution tabled by Mr ALMIRANTE and others on the situation in Eritrea (Doc. 1-45/83),
— *having regard* to the report of the Political Affairs Committee and the opinion of the Committee on Development and Cooporation (Doc. 1-1532/83),

1. OJ No. C 140, 5.6.1979, p. 82
2. OJ No. C 4, 7.1.1980, p. 75
3. OJ No. C 147, 16.6.1980, p. 120
4. OJ No. C 197, 4.8.1980, p. 81
5. OJ No. C 334, 20.12.1982, p. 84
6. OJ No. C 128, 16.5.1983, p. 63

A   – *Bearing in mind* the fact that Djibouti, Ethiopia and Somalia are signatories to the Lomé Convention,

B   – *Noting* the political and economic links between some Member States and these countries,

C   – *Noting* the strategic importance of the Horn of Africa for both Western countries and the Eastern Bloc, being adjacent to the Arabian peninsula,

D   – *Concerned* about the 20-year-old conflict between the Ethiopian State and the Eritrean resistance, in which Ethiopia is being supported by many thousands of troops and military advisers from the Soviet Union, the German Democratic Republic, Cuba and South Yemen,

E   – *Recalling* the resolution adopted by the Assembly of the United Nations on 2 December 1950 which stated that Eritrea should constitute an autonomous unit federated with Ethiopia and having wide powers over its own internal affairs,

F   – *Concerned* also about the Tigrai conflict and the guerilla war in the Ogaden,

G   – *Concerned* about the danger of a fragmentation of the Ethiopian State which might render the region of the Horn of Africa and surrounding areas even more unstable,

H   – *Alarmed* by the growing large-scale militarization of the region of the Horn of Africa, aggravated by Ethiopian policies and military action,

I   – *Concerned* about the tripartite agreement between Ethiopia, Libya and South Yemen which is foisting outside tensions into the region of the Horn of Africa,

J   – *Recalling* the resolution of the Foreign Ministers at the Islamic Conference in Islamabad in 1980, which called for the withdrawal of Soviet and allied troops from the region and also the removal of foreign bases in the Horn of Africa and the Red Sea and the exclusion of this area from superpower confrontation,

K   – *Disturbed* at the tension which exists between Ethiopia and her neighbours,

L   – *Critical* of the Ethiopian Government for its refusal to take part in the Nairobi meeting with the Sudanese Government, scheduled for 12 March 1984 and designed to settle the dispute between Ethiopia and the Sudan,

M   – *Deeply disturbed* at the renewed outbreak of revolt in the Southern region of the Sudan, fuelled also by hostile countries, and at the bombing of the Sudanese city of Omdurman on 16 March 1984,

N   – *Keenly concerned* abou the drought and famine afflicting the peoples of Ethiopia, Somalia and Djibouti,

O   – *Greatly alarmed* by the plight of refugees in the Horn of Africa and neighbouring countries such as the Sudan,

P   – *Stressing the fact* that Community aid, particularly food aid, contributed largely by ensuring the survival of the peoples of that area, who were the victims of drought and political conflicts simultaneously,

Q – *Pointing out* that the European Parliament delegation which went to the area in June 1983 noted that aid, particularly food aid, is being properly used in Ethiopia, Djibouti and Somalia,

R – *Stressing the need* for the Community to continue, if not to step up, its cooperation in the development of those countries, thereby contributing to stabilizing the region,

S – *Considering* that the tripartite agreement between Ethiopia, Djibouti and the United Nations High Commissioner on the repatriation of Ethiopian refugees in Djibouti should not lead to forcible repatriation,

T – *Disturbed* by the consequences of the creation of semi-permanent refugee camps in the Ogaden,

U – *Concerned* about the human rights situation in the region, particularly in Ethiopia,

V – *Alarmed* at the population explosion in the countries of the Horn of Africa and neighbouring regions (annual growth rates for 1970-1980 were: Ethiopia 2%, Somalia 2.8%, Djibouti 8.6%, Sudan 3.1%, Kenya 4%), which in the medium term will make the living conditions of these populations still worse and may reduce the effectiveness of the essential aid given by the European Community and the international community,

1. *Strongly condemns* the multiple interventions of the Soviet Union and the countries of the Eastern Bloc in the Horn of Africa and the stationing and use in action of troops from the Soviet Union, Cuba, the German Democratic Republic and South Yemen,

2. *Invites* all the great powers not to make this region a place of confrontation and rearmament,

3. *Asks* the Foreign Ministers meeting in political cooperation and the Council of Ministers as such:

    (a) to adopt a common standpoint on the problems of the Horn of Africa in order to take all such initiatives as may contribute to a solution of the conflicts and re-establishment of friendly relations between the states and the ethnic groups of the region,

    (b) to bring pressure to bear on the Soviet Union to withdraw its troops and those of countries allied to it from Ethiopia and to work together with the international community to aid the refugees and the people threatened by famine,

    (c) to strongly urge the Ethiopian Government to find a peaceful and negotiated solution of the conflict between it and the Eritrean peoples which takes account of their identity, as recognized by the United Nations resolution of 2 December 1950, and is consistant with the basic principles of the OAU,

    (d) to invite the Governments of Ethiopia, Somalia and Kenya to find peaceful solutions to their territorial and ethnic differences in such a way as to take account of the legitimate interests of the populations,

(e)   to bring all possible pressure to bear on the governments of the states of the region to respect human rights,

(f)   to ask, in particular, the Government of Ethiopia to release or bring to trial the former Royal family of Ethiopia, bearing in mind that the peoples of Europe, who attach great importance to respect for human rights, are providing substantial amounts of aid to promote the development of the countries of the Horn of Africa and to help meet the needs of the peoples of the area;

4.   *Calls on* the European Community, in the consultation with the UNHCR, to take active measures to solve the problems of the refugees in the region as proposed by the delegation of the European Parliament in June 1983;

5.   *Calls on* the Commission to maintain and increase its food aid for the countries of the region, including Sudan, and for the peoples of Eritrea and Tigray, both of them being severely affected not only by drought and famine, but also by military conflict, and to ensure that the means of its distribution are improved;

6.   *Invites* the European Community to do all in its power to help Ethiopia, Somalia and the United Nations High Commissioner for Refugees to reach a tripartite agreement on the voluntary repatriation of Ethiopian refugees in Somalia;

7.   *Asks* the Commission of the European Communities to take all necessary steps to ensure that the humanitarian aid granted reaches all the people affected, irrespective of their political sympathies;

8.   *Instructs* its President to forward this resolution to the Council, the Commission, the Foreign Ministers meeting on political cooperation, the Governments of the Member States, the parliaments of the Member States, the United Nations High Commissioner for Refugees and the Governments of Ethiopia, Somalia and Djibouti.

Appendix 9

BRITAIN FOREIGN OFFICE PAPER OF 3 DECEMBER 1890: SOUTHERN BOUNDARIES OF ABYSSINIA

CONFIDENTIAL

(6003.)

What are the Southern Boundaries of Abyssinia?

Memorandum respecting the Southern Boundaries of Abyssinia.

[WITH TWO MAPS]

'Gazetteer of the World,' 1878.
'Imperial Gazetteer,' 1886.
'Africa' (Keith Johnston), 1880.
'Encyclopædia Britannica,' 1875.

NEITHER the southern boundary of Abyssinia, nor that of the Kingdom of Shoa, which lies to the south-east of Abyssinia, are accurately defined in the Gazetteers and other English geographical works, which merely state that Abyssinia is bounded on the south by the country of the Gallas; while the southern and western boundaries of Shoa are mentioned as 'merely nominal, being from time to time pushed farther and farther into the adjoining countries.'

It should be here observed that when the term 'Galla tribes' only is mentioned, it is difficult to define their locality, as tribes bearing that name exist to the north and north-west of Shoa, as well as to the south-west, south, and south-east.

State Papers, vol. xlix, p. 808.

Consul Plowden stated in 1854 that: 'On the west and to the south-west vast forests frequented by wild beasts, or hot plains inhabited by negro races, exclude Abyssinia from the navigable part of the Blue Nile. *To the south* of that river an impetuous torrent forms its boundary, almost its safety, from the Gallas.'

8vo., 4247.

In the Map illustrating Dr. Beke's letters on Abyssinia in 1861, the River Abäi, or Upper Blue Nile, forms the south-western boundary of Abys-

99

sinia, while the Kingdom of Shoa extends southwards to about 9° north latitude.

The tribes which have been marked by Messrs.
Stanford on the accompanying Map as being
tributary to Shoa* were apparently independent
at the time of Captain Harris' mission to that
country in 1841, and also in 1854, when Consul
Plowden drew up his long Report of Abyssinia;
and it would appear that up to comparatively
recent times the Abäi formed the south-western,
and the Kingdom of Shoa the south-eastern
boundary of Abyssinia, while Shoa extended
southwards nearly as far as Lake Zooay.**

In 1856, when King Theodore reduced the
King of Shoa to be his tributary, he appears to
have vanquished several of the Galla tribes in the
neighbourhood of IIurrur,† but these conquests
were probably not of long duration, as in 1878,
when King Menelek of Shoa addressed letters to
the Queen and the German Emperor respecting
his desire to obtain unrestricted communication
with certain ports on the Red Sea, the German
missionaries who translated and forwarded the
respective letters observed, in so doing, 'that it
was requisite for the maintenance of tranquillity,
especially at the frontiers, to maintain a considerable army, and to take an offensive position
towards the powerful still unconquered heathen
Galla tribes in the south.'

The King stated, in his letter to the Queen,
that he had 'released all Galla prisoners taken in
war by his army, at one time 50,000, at another
20,000 souls,' and it would appear from the
authorities‡ hereafter quoted that it was about
this time that both Abyssinia and Shoa made considerable inroads on the Gallas, and that although
their southern frontiers may be said to have been

Map of the Nile, showing the
boundary between Italy and the
East Africa Company (Stanford).

Harris' 'Highlands of Ethiopia,'
8vo., 4387, vol. iii, p. 53.

State Papers, vol. xlix, pp. 849-854.

Petermann, 1867.

State Papers, vol. lii, pp. 845-852.

Confidential No. 4082, pp. 1-8.

* Mr. Bolton, Mr. Stanford's Geographer, has been asked
on what authority these tribes were marked as tributary to
Shoa, but he is unable to produce it.

** In most Maps Lake Zooay is placed just to the north of
the 8th parallel of north latitude, though in others it is situated
a little to the south of that parallel.

† ? Harrar.

‡ Those that are not Italian appear to have obtained their
information from Italian sources.

floating for some years previously according to the fortune of war, it is stated by some of these authorities that Shoa now claims as tributary the Galla tribes as far south as, and inclusive of, Kaffa, and that the tribes to the south of Godjam are claimed as tributary by the King of that province; while on the other hand Professor Fasolo alludes to the country of the Gallas as being still practically unexplored.

Map: Africa 126, small size.

The following is a translation of an extract from 'L'Abissinia Settentrionale,' by Captain A. Cecchi, published at Milan in 1888:

'The changes of frontiers caused by the vicissitudes of wars and conquests have for a long time prevented a precise political individuality being given to the name of Abyssinia. In a general way, however, the following boundaries may be at present given to that country. . . .

'To the west the plains of Sennaar and of Fazocle, which separate Abyssinia from the Nile. . .

'To the south its extent is undefined, as it depends on the fortune of the arms of Abyssinia in their annual wars against the restless Galla populations.

'The boundaries being uncertain, it is impossible to estimate its area with precision; however, it is approximately given as being actually (including the bordering territories of Galla) an extent of about 504,000 square centim., larger than that of Italy and her isles by 217 square centim., having also a population of about 7,600,000 inhabitants.

'Abyssinia is now politically divided into two Kingdoms, and into two vast Principalities.

'The Kingdoms are that of Shoa and that of Goggiam.*

'The Principalities are that of Tigrè and that of Amharia.

'The King of Shoa is Menelek II. The King of Goggiam is Tekla-Haimanot I.

'The Principality of Tigrè is governed by Ras Alula.

'In Amharia (a much vaster Principality) the Emperor Johannes III resides, and rules over it

* Godjam.

101

by means of some Ras, directly dependent on him.

'Of course Menelek, Tekla-Ilaimanot, and more especially Ras Alula, are subject to the Emperor, who is the King of Kings of Ethiopia (Negus-Neghest).

'The Kingdoms and Principalities in their turn are divided into provinces.

'Each province is administered by a Governor (Ras and Degiac-Mac), and is divided into districts, which are subdivided into smaller fractions governed by Seium (kind of Mayors).'

Professor Fasolo states in a work published in 1887 that:

'Abyssinia and the Italian Colonies on the Red Sea,' by Professor F. Fasolo, Caserta, 1887. P. 7.

'This region' (Abyssinia) 'is comprised between the 8° 32' and the 16° of north latitude and 35° and 40° 30' of east longitude (meridian of Paris).

'Its boundaries are ill-defined, especially to the east and west. On the north it has Nubia; on the west the as yet little-known countries of Gedaref and Galabat; on the south-west and the south the countries, at present practically unexplored, of the Gallas; on the east, Harrar, Adel, and the mountain districts approaching the Red Sea near Massowah.

'In the extreme south-west, surrounded by the Abäi, or Blue Nile, lies Goggiam; in the extreme south-east, surrounded by the Hawash, lies Shoa. To the south of these two regions are the countries of Liben, Guraghe, Guma, Limmu, Gimma, Ghera, and Sidama, among the Gallas.

P. 11.

'He' (King Menelek) 'was for ten years prisoner of King Theodore, when he managed to escape, and reconquered Shoa. In his kingdom he established freedom of worship, abolished slavery (nominally), and discomfited the Mahommedan tribes of the Gallas.'

P. 200.

In the Map attached to this work Abyssinia and Godjam are bounded on the south by the River Abäi, and Shoa by the River Hawash, about 8° 30' north latitude, while the Galla tribes to the south are not marked as being tributary to any State.

The Italian Geographical Society published a

'Bolletino della Società Geografica Italiana,' vol. xxiii, Serica 2, vol. xi (1886), p. 512.

Tracing of Map annexed.

Map in 1886 to illustrate the routes taken by the Italian travellers Cecchi and Chiarini, on which Map territories are not only marked as tributary to Shoa as far south 6° 45' north latitude, but are also parcelled out into different provinces.

This Map accompanies an article in which it is stated that, in consequence of the capture of Captain Cecchi by one of the smaller Galla States, King Menelek attacked and overthrew the Galla States in the south of Abyssinia; and that, in order to make his conquests lasting, he had united them to his kingdom, and appointed Governors over them.

With regard to the Map, the Italian Geographical Society observes: 'Captain Cecchi writes to us to point out the exact boundary between the territories which are tributary to Menelek and those which are dependent on King Tecla-Haimanot (formerly Ras Adul), a Goggiam.[*]

' "I know" (says the worthy traveller) "that Soddo-Galla, Cabièna, Guraghè, Tadallié, Botòr, Ciòra, Limmù, Gimma, Gomma, Ghera, and Caffa, that is to say, all the tribes which belong to the basin of the Ghibié, are tributaries of Menelek.

' "On the other hand, a good number of the inhabitants of the basin of the Diddesa, and one side of that of the Abäi, that is to say, Gudrù, Horrò-Galla, Liben-Galla, Gimma-Rare, Lagamarà, Gimma-Hine, and some tribes of the Sciancallà dwelling on the banks of the River Baro, pay tribute to King Tecla-Haimanot." '

This description is followed by a copy of a letter addressed by King Menelek to the Geographical Society of Rome in 1877, which bears the following heading:

'From Menelek II, King of Shoa, *Caffa, and all the confines of the country of the Gallas,* in the hope that it may reach the Head of the Geographical Society.'

The letter informs the Society that the Galla country is divided up amongst the Governors of his kingdom, and that every facility will be afforded to Italian travellers in those territories.

[*] Godjam.

In 1885, King Menelek, in according permission to Dr. Traversi to wander over all his territories, said that his country was so vast that he could go where no other European had ever been, as it was no longer as in the days of Cecchi, for the Galla were conquered, &c.

'Bolletino della Società Geografica Italiana,' 1889, p. 705.

In the Map attached to Petermann's Geography for 1867, the Abäi forms the south-western boundary of Abyssinia, and the Kingdom of Shoa extends a little to the south of Lake Zooay, or to about 8° 30' north latitude; but on a Map published in 1886, a rough tracing of which is annexed, territories are marked as tributary to Shoa as far south as Kaffa, or about 6° 45' north latitude.

Petermann, 1867.

Ibid., 1886.

This Map was issued to illustrate the route taken by the Italian travellers Cecchi and Chiarini, and the article which accompanies it gives similar information to that contained in the article in the 'Bolletino della Società Geografica Italiana,' alluded to above, which it quotes as its authority.

In March 1884 a paper was read by Mr. Ravenstein, at a meeting of the Royal Geographical Society, on 'Somal and the Galla Land,' which embodied information which had been collected by the Rev. Thomas Wakefield, who had lately travelled in those territories. In this paper Mr. Ravenstein said: 'Since this enterprising and arduous expedition (Cecchi-Chiarini), King John and his Viceroy Menelek of Shoa have extended their sway to the south as far as Kaffa; and the first European to avail himself of the facilities for travel thus afforded has been M. Soleillet, who visited Kaffa in 1882.'

Proceedings of the Royal Geographical Society, 1884, p. 258.

The following extracts are taken from the 'Nouvelle Géographie Universelle' (Reclus), and the 'Atlas de Géographie Moderne' (Hachette):

'Les Divisions Administratives et Politiques de l'Abyssinie changent à l'infini, suivant le pouvoir des feudataires et le caprice des Souverains.'

'Nouvelle Géographie Universelle' (E. Reclus), 1885, 8vo., 5688, vol. x, p. 287.

*　*　*　*　*

'Actuellement l'Empire d'Éthiopie, sans le royaume vassal du Choa, les États tributaires d'outre-Abaï,* les territoires récemment annexés au nord et les districts du Galla, comprend les provinces au plutôt les régions naturelles suivantes, classées en zones de climat et par bassins fluviaux.'

*   *   *   *   *

Ibid., p. 289.

'Le Choa ou Chawâ et les pays montagneux des Galla du nord font partie des plateaux Éthiopiens; au point de vue politique, le Choa, après avoir été longtemps indépendant, s'est rattaché de nouveau à l'Empire d'Abyssinie, et lui paye un tribut régulier. C'est la pierre au cou que le Souverain de Choa se présente devant le Roi des Rois.'

'Au sud de l'Abäi, des expéditions heureuses ont soumis la plupart des tribus, civilisées ou barbares, à l'Éthiopie du nord, et chaque année des Ambassades portent à Debra-Tabor ou à Makalé de l'ivoire ou des denrées précieuses.

'*De ce côté, des frontières flottantes, pour ainsi dire, enferment déjà toute l'Éthiopie méridionale jusqu'au delà du Kaffa;*' le Choa a triplé en étendue, et le Royaume de Godjam s'est accru dans la même proportion, quoique pendant sept ou huit mois de l'année l'Abäi séparc de l'Abyssinie les pays des Ilm-Orma.'

'Atlas de Géographie Moderne', (Hachette), 1890.

'*L'Éthiopie comprend l'Abyssinie, le Choa, ainsi que le Kaffa et autres pays tributaires du Choa.*'

On the Map the territories of Shoa are given as extending as far south as 6° north latitude.

8vo., 6695, 1888.

Mr. A. B. Wylde makes the following statement in his work on the Soudan, and although he quotes no authority, it appears to coincide with the accounts given by the Italian Geographical Society and by Petermann:

'King John is now King of Kings of all Abyssinia, and the territory over which he rules is well defined in the north, east, and west.

'The southern parts of his dominions are vague, but it is *supposed* that through King Menelek of Shoa, and King Tchlaihaimanout of the south-western Gallas, his power extends *nominally* through nearly the whole of the Galla country.

'There is no doubt that the conquests of King Tchlaihaimanout increase every season, and that he is working his way more and more every year to the south-west. . . .

* Tributary to the Blue Nile.

'King Menelek regions over the Shoa district, with his capital at Ankober.

'King Tchlaihaimanout's district extends from the south of Lake Tsana into the Galla country, following the Blue Nile River till it strikes the low country to the west, and then south to the Limou, Gimon, and Bagafar Gallas. He is also Vice-King of Godjam Province.

'King Tchlaihaimanout was known before as Ras Adul, and is descended in the female line from the old Kings of Abyssinia.'

Since the above work was written, Menelek of Shoa has defeated King John, and is now King of Abyssinia.

In the Map of Africa drawn up by the Intelligence Department of the Italian War Office, showing the possessions, Protectorates, and zones of influence of the different Powers on the African Continent, Abyssinia and Shoa are coloured as belonging to Italy as far south as the 5th parallel of north latitude until Shoa reaches the Juba. *The Marquis of Dufferin, No. 182, October 30, 1890.*

It will be observed that the information tending to show that Shoa has extended its sway as far south as inclusive of Kaffa, has been taken principally from Italian sources, and more especially from the travels of Cecchi and Chiarini, the former of whom only appears to have travelled as far as the northern borders of Kaffa, or to about 7° 15' north latitude, and though Mr. Ravenstein mentions that M. Soleillet visited Kaffa in 1882, we possess no record of his proceedings. *Royal Geographical Society, 1884, p. 258.*

It may be mentioned in conclusion that very little information respecting the southern boundaries of Abyssinia is contained, so far as I have been able to ascertain, in the Foreign Office archives, although there is a considerable amount of correspondence respecting the boundaries between Egypt and Abyssinia in the north, &c. as well as with regard to the proceedings of the Italians in the east.

FREDK. H. T. STREATFEILD

Foreign Office,
November 12, 1890.

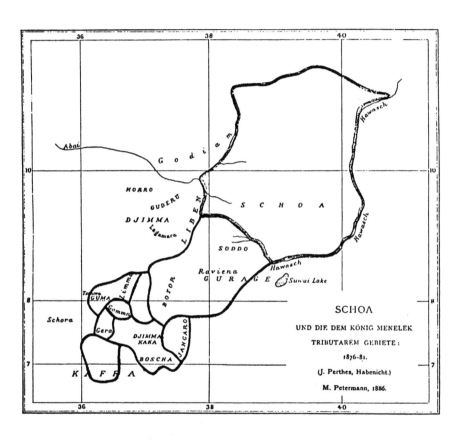

SCHOA
UND DIE DEM KÖNIG MENELEK
TRIBUTAREM GEBIETE:
1876-81.
(J. Perthes, Habenicht.)
M. Petermann, 1886.

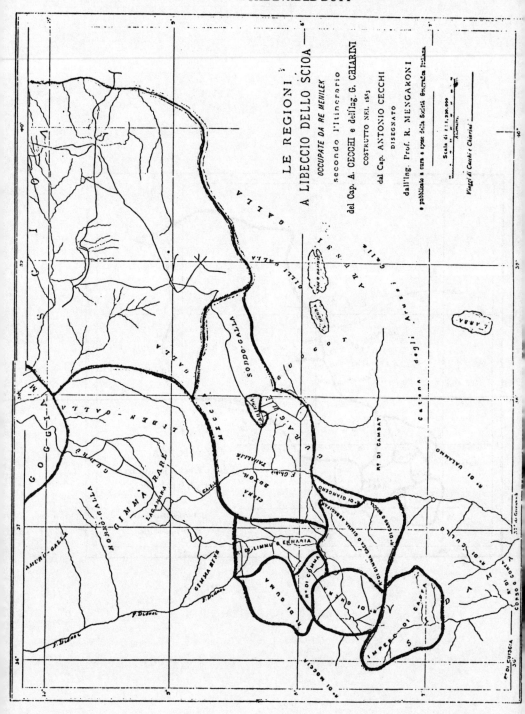

Appendix 10

FOREIGN OFFICE ARCHIVES, FILE REFERENCE
FO.1/32 & 33, CONCERNING THE *MISSION OF
MR. J. RENNELL RODD TO KING MENELEK IN 1897.*

**1. Extracts from the draft instructions given by Lord Salisbury, the British
Foreign Minister, to Mr. J. Rennell Rodd**

'. . . . . . .

'It must also carefully be borne in mind that Her Majesty's Government cannot pronounce upon any claims which the Italian Govt. may wish to advance to districts lying within the sphere of influence assigned to Italy by the Protocols of March 24 and April 15 1891 and of May 5 1894. H.M. Govt. have no exact information as to the intentions of the Italian Govt. in this respect and in view of the fact that the negotiations for the delimitation of frontier between Abyssinia and Italy provided for in the Treaty of Oct 26 1896 are still pending; it will be necessary that any arrangement which you may make in regard to the recognition of Abyssinian territorial claims should contain an explicit statement that such recognition is made only so far as British and Egyptian rights are concerned, and that any language that might be construed as a claim to dispose of the rights or reject the claims of other countries should be carefully avoided.

'The question of the frontiers of Abyssinia to the South West and South is one which may be more properly left for discussion between King Menelek and the Govt. of Italy within whose sphere of influence as recognised by Gt. Britain in the protocol of March 24 1891 those frontiers would seem to lie.

'You are not however precluded from listening to any statements which may be made to you of Abyssinian claims in this direction though it would be desirable to avoid placing them on record in any written agreement.

'With regard to the frontier on the S.E. you are aware that Ras Makanan who holds the Government of Harrar under King Menelek has advanced claims to the country occupied and governed by the GADABURSI tribe which lies within the present limits of the British Protectorate on the Somali Coast. The views of the Govt. of India as regards the conditions which may be agreed to on the settlement of of [sic] the frontier between Abyssinia and the British Protectorate are stated in the letter from the India Office of the 25 Jany. last, [. . . .]
' . . . .

'You will remember that one of the principal objects of your Mission is to come to arrangements with King Menelek for a definite understanding as to the frontier between Abyssinia and the Protectorate and for friendly inter-course and relations between the British and Abyssinian authorities and the inhabitants [illegible].

'You are authorised, if absolutely necessary, to make concessions in regard to the frontiers of the Protectorate as defined in the Protocol signed with Italy on the 5 May /94 provided such concessions are not of a nature to interfere with the main object for which the Protocol was assumed, viz: the securing of adequate supplies for the support of Aden, and the administration of the Pro-tectorate itself on a basis which shall as far as possible be at least self-support-ing, and should afford some prospect of the further development of the resources of the country. You will state that H.M. Govt. are ready to offer every facility in trade and commerce from Abyssinia through the Protectorate to the Sea Coast and that H.M.G. are ready to agree that all goods coming to or from Abyssinia for the use of the King or the Authes shall pass through Zeila free of duty. . . If you should find it absolutely necessary for the success of your negotiations you are authorized to concede the passage free of duty through Zeila of all goods coming to or going from Abyssinia, subject only to such dues as may fairly be charged for landing facilities and storage. Her Majesty's Govt. would however be very reluctant to cede to Abyssinia the port of Zeila. . .

'In the event of your finding it necessary for the purpose of your negotiations to agree to the transfer to Abyssinia of any of the tribes now under British pro-tection, you will be careful to obtain pledges that they will be treated with jus-tice and consideration. It will be essential that in your discussions and in any eventual agreement upon this point you should bear in mind the terms of the Protocol signed with Italy on May 5th/94 and that any recognition of the ter-ritorial claims of Abyssinia outside the British sphere of influence as defined in that Protocol, should be made on behalf of Gt. Britain alone without assuming to deal with claims or rights of other Powers.

'You will equally bear in mind that the Protocol in question precludes H.M. Govt. from attempting to include under British administration any country lying outside the British sphere of influence as defined in it. Finally it will be necessary to take account of the notes exchanged between the British and French Govts. in February 1888 with regard to their respective Protectorates on the Somali Coast. The provisions laid down in those notes are still in force and must be carefully observed.

' . . . .

'You may assure King Menelek that wherever the possessions of the two countries are close to one another, we shall prefer that our frontiers should be coterminous and if you can procure an assurance that districts recognized by us as Abyssinian shall not be ceded to other Powers it would be desirable that you should do so.

' . . . . . '

2. Extracts from Despatch No. 14 from Mr. Rennell Rodd to Lord Salisbury

Adis Abbaba,
May 3rd, 1897

'My Lord,
    'I have the honour to report that in the course of negotiations with the King respecting the future boundaries of the Somali Coast Protectorate, I asked His Majesty whether any definite delimitation of the French Hinterland to the Gulf of Tajourah had been arrived at. The King said he would show me the line that had been agreed upon with Monsieur Lagarde at his recent visit to Adis Abbaba. As however the map upon which the line had been traced was not immediately forthcoming, he instructed Monsieur Ilg to call in the afternoon and explain to me the boundary that had been agreed upon.

    'Monsieur Ilg pointed out a line on the Italian map (Carta dimostrativa dell'Ethiopia. Sections Abbab and Harrar) which, starting from the Coast, South of Raheita runs nearly due West to Rasa. Thence turning South west it runs directly to the East end of Lake Vadaraibaito. From there it is drawn in an arc which skirting the Easternmost point of Lake Abbe ends at Gobbad. From Gobbad the line runs East South East to Gialelo a little north of Abbasouen on the boundary fixed by agreement between Great Britain and France in Feb 1888.
'   . . . .

    'The exact text of the arrangement I have not been able to obtain.

'I have (etc.)
'Rennell Rodd'

3. Extracts from Despatch No. 15 from Mr. Rennell Rodd to Lord Salisbury

Adis Abbaba
4th May, 1897

'   . . . . .

    'His Majesty [King Menelek] answered that it referred to a circular letter which he had addressed on the 10th of April 1891 to the Sovereigns and Chiefs of the various States of Europe in which he laid down that he considered the actual boundaries of the present Ethiopian Empire to be, and further defined what may by analogy be described as a sphere of influence, including all the territories that had at any time in the past been tributary to Ethiopia, and which it was his avowed intention to bring once more within the area of his dominions. . . The line actually laid down by King Menelek actually cuts off the greater portion of the British Protectorate of Somaliland leaving a narrow strip along the sea. . . '

111

4. Enclosure to Despatch No. 15 (above), being a translation of the Circular letter addressed by King Menelek to the Heads of State of Britain, France, Germany, Italy and Russia in 1891

'Being desirous to make known to our friends the Powers (Sovereigns) of Europe the boundaries of Ethiopia, we have addressed also to you (your Majesty) the present letter.

'These are the boundaries of Ethiopia:–

'Starting from the Italian boundary of Arafale, which is situated on the sea, the line goes westward over the plain (Meda) of Gegra towards Mahio, Halai, Digsa, and Gura up to Adibaro. From Adibaro to the junction of the Rivers Mareb and Arated.

'From this point the line runs southward to the junction of the Atbara and Setit Rivers, where is situated the town known as Tomat.

'From Tomat the frontier embraces the Province of Gedaref up to Karkoj on the Blue Nile. From Karkoj the line passes to the junction of the Sobat River with the White Nile. From thence the frontier follows the River Sobat, including the country of the Arbore, Gallas, and reaches Lake Samburu.

'Towards the east are included within the frontier the country of the Borana Gallas and the Arussi country up to the limits of the Somalis, including also the Province of Ogaden.

'To the northward the line of frontier includes the Habr Awaz, the Gadabursi, and the Esa Somalis, and reaches Ambos.

'Leaving Ambos the line includes Lake Assal, the province of our ancient vassal Mohamed Anfari, skirts the coast of the sea, and rejoins Arafale.

'While tracing to-day the actual boundaries of my Empire, I shall endeavour, if God gives me life and strength, to re-establish the ancient frontiers (tributaries) of Ethiopia up to Khartoum, and as far as Lake Nyanza with all the Gallas.

'Ethiopia has been for fourteen centuries a Christian island in a sea of pagans. If Powers at a distance come forward to partition Africa between them, I do not intend to be an indifferent spectator.

'As the Almighty has protected Ethiopia up to this day, I have confidence He will continue to protect her, and increase her borders in the future. I am certain He will not suffer her to be divided among other Powers.

'Formerly the boundary of Ethiopia was the sea. Having lacked strength sufficient, and having received no help from Christian Powers, our frontier on the sea coast fell into the power of the Mussulman.

'At present we do not intend to regain our sea frontier by force, but we trust that the Christian Power, guided by our Saviour, will restore to us our sea-coast line, at any rate, certain points on the coast.

'Written at Adis Abbaba, the 14th Mazir, 1883 (10th April, 1891).

'(Translated direct from the Amharic.)

'Adis Abbaba, 4th May, 1897.'

5. Despatch No. 18 from Mr. Rennell Rodd to Lord Salisbury

Adis Abbaba,
May 9th 1897

contains a Memorandum by Lt. Col. Wingate and Capt. Count Gleichen describing the limits of the Ethiopian Empire and the territories actually under effective occupation.

6. Extracts from Memorandum enclosed with Despatch No. 18 (above) being the Memorandum of Lt. Col Wingate and Capt. Count Gleichen describing the limits of the Ethiopian Empire under effective occupation

'
  . . . . .

'*S & S.E. Frontiers*	'The South and South Eastern Frontiers of Abyssinia as defined in Menelek's Proclamation are stated to include the country of the BORANA GALLAS and the ARUSSI country up to the limits of the SOMALIS including also the Province of OGADEN. From information gathered here there would appear to be little doubt that the greater part of these countries are now more or less effectively occupied by the Abyssinians.
'*RAS WALDA GABRIEL'S Province*	The Governor of these provinces is RAS WALDA GABRIEL who occupied the town of LOGH on the JUBA river – some 250 miles from KISMAYU – on 30 July 1895, as well as the town of BARI on the WEBBE SHEBELYI – about the same distance from the coast as LOGH. As however, these places lie in the plains in which the Abyssinians find it difficult to live owing to climatic reasons, WALDA GABRIEL has established his headquarters in the higher regions at KARANLE in the district of IME from whence he despatches from time to time expeditions into the lower countries to raid and collect taxes.
'*E. Frontier*	'The terms of the Proclamation are very vague as to the actual Abyssinian boundaries on the Eastern frontier, and, as far as can be ascertained here, the countries in question have been so recently occupied that it is at present impossible to define the actual limits of Menelek's authority in these directions, but here, as in the South-Eastern frontier, raids on a large scale from the mountainous districts into the maratime [sic] plains would appear to be the usual

methods by which the Abyssinians maintain their influence.

'N.E. Frontier

'As regards the North-Eastern boundaries, the Proclamation states that the Abyssinian frontier line includes the HABR AWAL, the GADABURSI, and the ESA SOMALIS and reaches AMBOS, whence, including Lake ASSAL and skirting the Coast line, it rejoins the Northern limits at ARAFLE.

'RAS MAKONAN'S Province

' . . . RAS MAKONAN . . . as Governor of the HARAR Province naturally considers within his sphere, those countries and tribes included within the British Protectorate as defined by the Anglo-Italian Protocol of 5th May 1894 of which the Abyssinian authorities ignore all knowledge on the grounds that this treaty has never been officially communicated to them by the Italian authorities. Apart, however from this fact Menelek was also in entire ignorance of British Protective treaties over the

'British Treaties with Somali tribes

MIJJERTAIN SOMALIS	dated	1st May 1884
HABR AWAL SOMALIS	dated	14th July 1884
GADABURSI SOMALIS	dated	11 Decr 1884
HABR TOLJAALA SOMALIS	dated	26 Decr 1884
ESA SOMALIS	dated	31 Decr 1884
HABR GERHAJIS SOMALIS	dated	13 Jany 1885
WARSANGALI SOMALIS	dated	27 Jany 1886
HABR TOLJAALA SOMALIS	dated	1st Feby 1886
HABR GERHAJIS SOMALIS	dated	1st Feby 1886
HABR AWAL SOMALIS	dated	15 March 1886

such Treaties having been concluded during and subsequent to the Egyptian occupation of HARAR and prior to the seizure of that Province by the Abyssinians.

'BIYO KABOBA

' . . . RAS MAKONAN has established a fort at BIYO KABOBA on the British side of the Frontier as defined by the Anglo-French Treaty of March 1888, and

'JIGJIGA

another at JIGJIGA which is just outside the British Frontier as defined by the Anglo-Italian Protocol of May 1894, and that, moreover the Abyssinian flag has been hoisted from time to time at ALALO within the GADABURSI country.

'The new French boundary in Abyssinia

'The Abyssinian authorities have also officially communicated to us that Mons. Legard, the French envoy, in his recent mission to the Emperor Menelek concluded with him a Treaty by which the

French sphere of influence on the JIBUTI neighbourhood is bounded by a line running due West from a point on the Coast line just South of RAHEITA to RASA, thence to LAKE WADAUIBAITO, whence it trends in a Southerly direction to GOBBAD and there turning Eastwards joins the British frontier (as established by the Anglo-French agreement of March 1888) at JAL-LELO. . . .

7. Extract from Despatch No. 20 from Mr. Rennell Rodd to Lord Salisbury

Addis Abbaba
13th May 1897

' . . . .

'The following morning I went again to the Palace, and resumed our discussions on the Somali Coast frontier, which I explained I did not feel able to define in an article, until we had somewhat cleared the ground by thoroughly understanding the basis of our respective claims. I drew attention to the fact that the declaration he had furnished me with (inclosure in my No. 15) lay claim to districts which cover more than half of our Protectorate as defined in an agreement, which we had every reason to believe would, under the Ucciali Treaty, as we at the time understood it, have been brought to his notice. That we had concluded Treaties dating from 1884 and 1886 with the Tribes included in that line and considered our Rights there fully established.

'Looking at the way on which the frontier was traced he exclaimed, but you are advancing right up to the gates of Harar.

'I pointed out that it was Abyssinia which had advanced up to us, that we were the reversionaries of Egypt in those districts, and had established ourselves there by treaties with the native tribes before the Abyssinians had come to Harar.

'The Emperor then again referred to the ancient limits of Ethiopia. I asked him how the Somalis who had been established in those regions for so many centuries could possibly be looked upon as included within the ancient limits of Ethiopia. His Majesty then propounded the extraordinary doctrine that the Somalis had been from time immemorial, until the Moslem invasion, the cattle keepers of the Ethiopians, who could not themselves live in low countries; they had had to pay their tribute of cattle to their masters and had been coerced when they failed to do so.

'I replied that we would not consider claims based on such grounds as this, that by all recognised international law it was the actual occupant that must be dealt with and we were, as I had already explained, the reversionaries of Egypt.

' "Then" said the Emperor Menelek, "accepting this View let me deal with you. What I should prefer, so as to give the French no grounds for complaining of differential treatment, is to draw a line parallel to the Coast, corresponding to that which I have agreed upon with them, namely about one hundred (100) kilometres in depth, and recognising all on the sea side as the British Protectorate".

'I pointed out in reply that such an arrangement would not be acceptable in our case, as the tribes in our Protectorate were for the most part pastoral and nomadic, changing their pastures according to the seasons, and in any arrangement to be made the habits and migrations of the tribes must be carefully studied before a line was fixed.

' . . . I then told him that I was ready to meet him in a spirit of concession. He complained of our proximity to Harar, I would suggest therefore cutting off the triangle included between Bia Kaboba, Gildessa and Makaris which would transfer the White Esa tribe to Ethiopia and remove the line of demarcation a good many marches further from Harar. I was also prepared to offer concessions on the Eastern side. But I considered the Gadaboursi and certain other tribes indispensable to us, in view of the main object for which our Protectorate is maintained I should mention that the concessions were proposed after due discussion with Captain Swayne. The tribes in the Eastern part of the Protectorate are, he reports, at present practically out of our control, while the White Esa, since the erection of the Abyssinian fort which has been suffered to remain for 6 or 7 years at Bia Kaboba, had practically been living under the shadow of Abyssinian influence.

'I then submitted an English and Amharic text of certain articles, securing liberty to British subjects to enter and trade in Ethiopia, maintaining the Zeyla Harrar route open to commerce, giving His Majesty faculty to appoint a representative at Zeyla, and asking for most favoured nation treatment for Great Britain and her colonies.

' . . . . .

'Finally we reopened the question of the definition of the frontiers of the frontiers of the [sic] Somali Coast Protectorate. I recapitulated the whole situation, the misunderstandings which had arisen owing to our not realising each others' point of departure, and once more urged on him a line based on tribal divisions on which indeed the line we had drawn in the Anglo-Italian Protocol of May 1894 was based. His Majesty's attitude was distinctly oriental. England was a great Power, could we not cede these small parcels of territory, which meant so little to us and so much to him? He had gained Harrar by conquest and looked on these regions as part and parcel of the Harrar Province. I assured him that this was not so, we were established in these countries long before the Expedition which resulted in his annexation of Harrar, and though he had conquered Harrar he had not conquered us. I showed him on the map the pastures frequented by the tribes under our protection, demonstrating that the line I proposed to draw with Captain Swayne's concurrence, was a reasonable and just division. But His Majesty replied he could not understand maps sufficiently to judge, should we not rather agree to maintain the status quo. I replied that the status quo must be defined in an agreement, for it was impossible to know what the actual conditions of occupation were, since Ras Makunan had hoisted a flag and raised a claim of jurisdiction at Alalo which we were unable to admit his right to do.

'   . . . . .

'I . . . suggested that he should empower Ras Mukunan to come to an agreement with me at Harrar which should be annexed to any Treaty we might sign, in the form of an exchange of notes. To this proposition he eventually consented on condition that the arrangement was submitted to him for approval, I claimed reciprocity in this respect and an article was accordingly framed in that sense.

'I would submit that this appeared to be the only way out of the impasse, for although my instructions on this point are large and liberal I could not see my way to accepting the arbitrary line proposed by the Emperor without endangering the main interest for which the Protectorate is maintained, and from our experience of the treatment which the Abyssinians mete out to their subject tribes, to which I have alluded elsewhere, I do not think anything but the most urgent necessity could justify handing over tribes who have known the advantages of British rule to the tender mercies of this marauding race.

'   . . . . .

'The failure to definitely settle here the question of the Somali Coast frontier was a great disappointment to me, but I trust that your Lordship will after perusing this despatch agree that a settlement here was only possible upon terms which I could not be justified in entertaining. I trust, at any rate, that the way has been paved for an arrangement, partly through clearing away misapprehensions and misunderstandings, and partly through the finding of a form of agreement which will greatly facilitate the final settlement.'

'   . . . . . '

8. Extracts from Despatch No. 35 from Mr. Rennell Rodd to Lord Salisbury

Harrar
June 4th, 1897

(being a Report on Rodd's negotiations with Ras Makunan)

'   . . . . .

'These negotiations which were concluded this morning have been throughout most wearing and trying . . . most of all on account of all very exorbitant nature of the Abyssinian pretensions and the theory they cling to that the dependencies of Harrar extended to the Sea.

'   . . . . .

'In view of the great difficulties I have had to encounter that the fact that I was practically without the means of exercising any moral pressure, while the French had but a few weeks ago accepted so conspicuous a curtailment of their protectorate claims on the Somali Coast, I trust that Your Lordship will consider that the arrangement is as satisfactory a one as we were entitled to except. Although considerable concessions from our original boundary line, as defined by the Anglo-Italian Protocol of May 1894, have been made. I think that the essential points drawn attention to in my instructions have been carefully safeguarded, and I do not believe that under the circumstances it would have been possible to secure more favourable conditions.

'　. . . . .

'I began by saying that the Emperor had on my taking leave of him explained that he had given the Ras instructions to be very conciliatory, and had assured me I should meet with no difficulties. I had, I said, proposed to him certain valuable concessions in view of his anxiety to remove the frontier further from Harrar of which he was no doubt aware, and I hoped it only remained for us to decide upon the precise Geographical line which should separate us and which the Emperor Menelek, in his ignorance of the country in question, had felt himself unable to fix. I then repeated to him the grounds on which our claims to these territories were based and said that while anxious to come to an amicable arrangement, we would not for a moment admit that there was any question to our title. It was here at the very outset that I perceived that logic or argument were entirely unprofitable and wasted, for the Ras after listening patiently, produced a small and very inaccurate Italian map on which a line was drawn in red chalk marking out a sphere about one hundred kilometres in depth parallel to the coast similar to that accepted by the French, and starting from the same point on the Zeyla-Harrar road. This, he said, was what the Emperor Menelek was prepared to accept as our boundary. It was in fact the line which the Emperor had spoken of at Adis Abbaba (see my despatch No. 20 of 13th ult.) with this difference, that instead of joining the sea at the 49th parallel it did so on the 48th, in virtue of my having spoken of offering concessions on the Eastern side, if my line on the Western were accepted.

'I at once told the Ras that I had long ago explained to the Emperor Menelek that I could not negotiate on such a basis and that I was much surprised at the proposal being brought up again.

'He then drew a line about half-way between this line and the boundary defined in the Anglo-Italian Protocol of May 1894, and suggested that this would fairly represent an equal division of reciprocal concession. In the discussion which ensued the Ras gave me to understand that this was all that he could do without reference to the Emperor, and it appeared as if we should not be able to get any further, as I was quite unprepared to consider a proposal of this kind, ignoring tribal limits and geographical conditions and disposing with a piece of red chalk of nearly half of our Protectorate. The Ras said he did not understand how we could claim as in our Protectorate regions where the subjects of Ethiopia were established, where they had posts and even forts. With regard to this last I said I supposed he meant Bia Caboba, that we had protested against the erection of the fort there, but were anxious not to come to any conflict and had only tolerated the Abyssinian flag there, while they were involved in other troubles, pending a solution at the proper time. Beyond an iteration of the statement Bia Caboba is ours, no argument appeared to make any impression. I promised however to consider before the following day whether I could find any basis for further negotiation in accepting a portion of this line on the

Western side but told him frankly that my proposals to make possible concessions on the Eastern side were entirely conditional on the acceptance of my original line between Bia Caboba and Makanis, and that if I was to make any further concessions on this side I must withdraw the suggestion entirely.

'I then discussed the question thoroughly with Captain Swayne and also with Captain Harrington the assistant political Resident at Zeyla who is thoroughly conversant with the local situation in the neighbourhood of the caravan Road and who had come to Harrar to meet us. The latter was naturally adverse to any arrangement which would interfere with the control over the Esa camel holders [sic] who came to load up at Zeyla, and we were all of us extremely reluctant to hand over to such masters as the Abyssinians any tribes who had been entitled to look for British protection however indirectly exercised. Nevertheless it was obvious that without our being prepared to assert our claims in some more convincing manner than we have hitherto done, or as far as I could judge from my instructions intend [sic] to do, any understanding would be impossible without much larger concessions that I had at first proposed to make. The Abyssinians were to some extent practically in the position of 'Beati possidentes', and while not actually wishing to risk a quarrel would undoubtedly push on gradually further and further, being the more encouraged to do so by the fact that their former encroachments had met with no material opposition.

'I therefore made up my mind to endeavour to recommence negotiations on the first part of the line, starting from the Zeyla-Harrar Road, and I found the Ras had admitted my contention that no concessions on the Western side could now be contemplated. I felt the more convinced of the necessity of adopting this position since I had meet [sic] Doctor Nerazzini on the road and had learned from him that the Italian Government did not intend to abandon the western sea board South of Cape Guardafni and will therefore remain our neighbours there. When I saw Ras Makunan on the following morning I was accompanied by Captain Swayne.

'The line proposed by Ras Makunan had started at Ellan on the Zeyla-Harrar Road. This is not a good point geographically and both Captain Swayne and Captain Harrington recommended in preference the hill or mountain of Somadou somewhat nearer Bia Caboba. This after very great difficulty was agreed to. The line was then drawn to about half way between the 9th and 10th parallel and the Ras had hoped when it came to defining it, I afterwards discovered, to be able to deflect it towards Hargeisa. My whole attention was directed on the contrary to bringing it further South without appearing to do so, by endeavouring to find good land marks with which to define it. And here our great difficulties began for the Ras had not the most elementary knowledge of geography or geographical expressions, nor did he know the country in question sufficiently well to be able to identify the places on the line. He had collected a few merchants and Somalis who frequent those parts to advise him but owing to the difference of pronunciation many of the names on the maps, which are only locally known could not be identified. . . . His great apprehension throughout was the proximity of any line we might be striving for to the fort of Jig-jiga. . . He fought desperately for Hargeisa. . .

'Now Hargeisa or Sheikh Mutta is in a way the sacred city of the Somalis who come to Berbera and to hand it over to the Abyssinians would mean to lose all influence and prestige with many of the tribes of great importance to us in view of the Aden food supply, which my instructions specially directed me to safeguard, whatever else might be abandoned. . . .

' . . . he abandoned the point reluctantly, murmuring that we were taking all the land that had any value and only giving him the desert, an observation which our experience of the Western side of Somali coast leads me to think is not without justification.

' . . . I succeeded in getting him to agree to a line starting at Somadou, passing through the Saw and Egu hills by Moga Medir on the edge of the Harrar prairie to Arran Arrhe at the intersection of the 44th meridian with the 9th parallel. The grazing rights being reserved to the occupants of either side of the line.

'From there the boundary is determined by a geographical line, drawn to the intersection of the 47th meridian with the 8th parallel. I tried very hard to bring the boundary from Arrhan Arrhe down to the Northernmost wells of Milmil, but the Ras on his side fought for the 9th parallel as the boundary line right away to its intersection with the 48th meridian, cutting off from us some of the best food supplying country to the West, and the negotiations appeared once more to be menaced, so that I agreed to a certain compromise which in Captain Swayne's opinion would not involve the abandonment of any districts of particular importance to us, so long as grazing rights and access to water on the far side of the line were secured. On the South of the new boundary line will be found a certain number of small tribes connected with the Ogadeyn while those connected with the Habr-Gerhaji, and in fact most of the tribes who go to Berbera are established to the North, and retained in the Protectorate.

'In accordance with my instructions it was necessary for me here as it had been in drafting article III of the Treaty to find a form which would only involve Abyssinian recognition of our protectorate without in any way admitting recognition on our part of a cession to Ethiopia.

'I had succeeded in doing this in the Treaty. . . On my pointing out however that it was best for us to abide by the form of expression laid down in the Treaty by the Emperor Menelek I succeeded in getting rid of any phraseology which necessarily implied a recognition of Abyssinian rights beyond our frontier.

'I hesitated for a moment over one other point, namely whether when the limit of the readjustment was reached it was prudent to refer to the Anglo-Italian protocol for a definition of the rest of the line. My instructions were to avoid any mention of the claims of Italy, but I found in the course of our discussions that the line of Anglo-Italian protocol was a recognised historical land mark and the Ras had frequently referred to it as indicating the furthest limit of British claims on the territory in question, so that it did not seem that I could incur the risk of opening any controversy by referring to it, and the regions beyond the British limit to the West appeared to be generally acknowledged as remaining under Italian influence. . . I therefore felt I should not be going beyond my instructions in merely referring to this document with which he was quite familiar and to which in this respect he made no objection.

' . . . . .

'I believe that with the reserves which are made with respect to grazing rights and access to wells, the actual conditions of the tribes on the borders of the new line will not be greatly modified, and that everything will go on very much as it does at present, but a bound will be set to the encroachments and raids of the Abyssinians which should produce in the long run a greater feeling of security among the populations retained under British protection. The greater part of the territory ceded comprises temporary grazing grounds not under permanent occupation.

' . . . I am of opinion therefore that the ceded strip will become a sort of neutral zone or buffer district.

'If the control over the Esa camel men who come to Zeyla seems weakened by the cession of the triangle between Bia Caboba, Gildessa and Makunis the danger is I think more apparent than real. . . .

'In any case I trust that Your Lordship will agree that the advantages of a definite settlement, which after all reserved to us the greater part of the sphere we had claimed and only abandons in sparsely populated and barren region will well outweigh any local difficulties which may arise.

' . . . It is scarcely possible to provide for all contingencies in a document which in order to be understood by savage or semi-savage people must be couched in the simplest possible terms.

' . . . Alalo will be excluded from and Lasmaan retained within the limits of the British Protectorate as recognised by Ethiopia'.

Appendix 11

NOTE FROM 'BRITISH AND FOREIGN STATE PAPERS', VOLUMES 76 AND 77, CONCERNING AGREEMENTS CONCLUDED BETWEEN BRITAIN AND VARIOUS SOMALI TRIBES 1884-1886.

1. Agreements published in Volume 76, pp. 99 *et seq.* are in the following terms:

'Treaties of Commerce &c. between Great Britain and Native Chiefs and States on the Somali Coast -1884, 1885
(included in "Correspondence respecting Ports in the Red Sea and the Gulf of Aden, and the Province of Harrar" laid before Parliament in 'Egypt No. 14, 1885')

Agreement with the Habr-Awal (Non-cession of Territory except to British Government, British Vessels allowed to trade at Berbera, Bulhar, &c; Slave Trade) – July 14, 1884

WHEREAS the garrisons of His Highness the Khedive are about to be withdrawn from Berbera and Bulhar, and the Somali Coast generally, we, the undersigned Elders of the Habr-Awal tribe, are desirous of entering into an Agreement with the British Government for the maintenance of our independence, the preservation of order, and other good and sufficient reasons;

Now it is hereby agreed and covenanted as follows:

ART. I. The Habr-Awal do hereby declare that they are pledged and bound never to cede, sell, mortgage, or otherwise give for occupation, save to the British Government, any portion of the territory presently inhabited by them, or being under their control.

II. [Vessels under British flag to have freedom to trade]

III. [British subjects to have safety, protection and safe conduct]

IV. [Traffic in slaves to cease]

V. The British Government shall have the power to appoint an Agent or Agents to reside at Berbera, or elsewhere in the territories of the Habr-Awal, and every such Agent shall be treated with respect and consideration, and be entitled to have for his protection such guards as the British Government deem sufficient.

The above-written Treaty shall come into force and have effect from the date on which the Egyptian troops shall embark at Berbera; but the Agreement shall be considered provisional, and subject to revocation or modification, unless confirmed by competent authority.

[Follows names of tribal signatories]

[14th July 1884]

F.M. HUNTER, Major
Officiating Political Resident,
Aden

Witness

Signatures marks or seals of
Elders

Witnesses
True Copy'

Note: Agreements in similar terms were made by Major F.M. Hunter with the Elders of the following tribes, on the dates indicated:-

Tribe	Date
The Gadabursi	11th December 1884
The Habr Toljaala	26th December 1884
The Eesa Somal	31st December 1884
The Habr Gerhajis	13th January 1885

2. Agreements published in Volume 77, pp. 1263 *et seq.* are in the following terms:–

'TREATIES, &c, between Great Britain and Native Chiefs and States on the Somali Coast, &c. – 1886

Agreements with the Warsangali (British Protection; Slave Trade; Wrecks; &c.) – January 27, 1886

The British Government and the Elders of the Warsangali tribe who have signed this Agreement being desirous of maintaining and strengthening the relations of peace and friendship existing between them;

The British Government have named and appointed Major Frederick Mercer Hunter, C.S.I., Political Agent and Consul for the Somali Coast, to conclude a Treaty for this purpose.

The said Major F.M. Hunter, C.S.I., Political Agent and Consul for the Somali Coast, and the said Elders of the Warsangali, have agreed upon and concluded the following Articles:

ART. I. The British Government, in compliance with the wish of the undersigned Elders of the Warsangali, undertakes to extend to them and to the territories under their authority and jurisdiction the gracious favour and protection of Her Majesty the Queen – Empress.

II. The said Elders of the Warsangali agree and promise to refrain from entering into any correspondence, Agreement, or Treaty with any foreign nation or Power, except with the knowledge and sanction of Her Majesty's Government.

III. [relates to assistance to vessels]

IV. [relates to traffic in slaves]

V. [relates to appointment of Agent by British]

VI. The Warsangali hereby engage to assist all British officers in the execution of such duties as may be assigned to them, and further to act upon their advice in matters relating to the administration of justice, the development of the resources of the country, the interests of commerce, or in any other matter in relation to peace, order and good government, and the general progress of civilisation.

VII. This Treaty to come into operation from the 27th day of January, 1886, on which date it was signed at Bunder Gori by the Undermentioned.

[signatures]

[sgd] DUFFERIN, Viceroy and Governor
General of India'

This Treaty was ratified by the Viceroy and Governor-General of India in Council at Simla on the 15th day of May, A.D. 1886

Note. Agreements in terms similar to Articles I, II and VI were made with the Habr Tojaala, and the Habr Gerhajis, both on 1 February, 1886; and with the Habr Awal on 15 March 1886.

Appendix 12

TREATIES AND AGREEMENTS 1897–1908

I. TREATY BETWEEN ITALY AND ABYSSINIA, SIGNED AT ADDIS
ABABA, 26 OCTOBER 1896

[Ratified by the King of Italy, 1 January 1897]

In the name of the Most Holy Trinity

His Majesty Umberto I, King of Italy, and His Majesty Menilek II, Emperor of Ethiopia, being desirous of ending the state of war and of reviving their former friendship, have concluded the following Treaty:

For the purpose of concluding this Treaty, His Majesty the King of Italy appointed, as his Envoy Plenipotentiary, Major Doctor Cesare Nerazzini, Knight of Saint Maurice and Saint Lazarus, Officer of the Crown of Italy. The full powers of Major Nerazzini having been found to be in good and due form, His Excellency Major Nerazzini, in the name of His Majesty the King of Italy, and His Majesty Menilek II, Emperor of Ethiopia and of the Galla Countries, in his own name, have met and agreed the following Articles:

Art. I.   –   [End of State of War. Perpetual Peace and Friendship.]
Art. II.   –   [Treaty of 2nd May, 1889, annulled]
Art. III.   –   [Recognition by Italy of Ethiopia as a Sovereign and Independent State]

Frontiers

Art. IV. – The two Contracting Powers having been unable to agree on the question of frontiers, but desiring to conclude a peace without delay and thus to bring to their Countries the benefits of peace, it has been agreed that within one year from today's date, Commissioners of His Majesty the King of Italy and of His Majesty the Emperor of Ethiopia will establish the definitive frontiers by mutual agreement. Until the frontiers have been thus fixed, the two Contracting Parties agree to observe the *statu quo ante*, and mutually refraining strictly from breaching the provisional frontier, delimited by the courses of the Mareb, Belessa, and Mouna Rivers.

125

Non-cession of Territory by Italy to any other Power

Art. V. – Until the Italian Government and the Ethiopian Government have by mutual agreement fixed their definitive frontiers, the Italian Government undertakes not to make any cession whatsoever of territory to any other Power. If the Italian Government of its own volition wishes to abandon a part of the territory which it holds, such territory will be transferred to Ethiopia.

Art. VI.   –   [Commercial Agreements to the concluded.]

Art. VII.   –   [Treaty to be brought to notice of other Powers.]

Art. VIII.   –   *Ratification of Treaty*

This Treaty shall be ratified by the Italian Government within three months of today's date.

Art. IX. – This Treaty of Peace concluded today shall be drawn up in Amharic and in French, the two texts being in absolute conformity, made in duplicate, signed by the two Parties; one copy shall remain in the hands of His Majesty the King of Italy and the other in the hands of His Majesty the Emperor of Ethiopia.

Being in agreement on the terms of this Treaty, His Majesty Menilek II, Emperor of Ethiopia, in his own name, and His Excellency Major Doctor Nerazzini, in the name of His Majesty the King of Italy, have approved the same and affixed their seals.

Done at Adis Abbaba, 17 Tekemt, 1889 (corresponding to 26 October 1896).

[L.S.] Major CESARE NERAZZINI,
Envoy Plenipotentiary of His
Majesty the King of Italy.

[Seal of His Majesty Emperor Menilek II.]

II. TREATY BETWEEN GREAT BRITAIN AND ETHIOPIA*

Signed by the Emperor Menelek II, and by Her
Majesty's Envoy, at Adis Abbaba, May 14, 1897

Ratified by the Queen, July 28, 1897

Her Majesty Victoria, by the grace of God, Queen of Great Britain and Ireland, Empress of India, and His Majesty Menelek II, by the grace of God, King of Kings of Ethiopia, being desirous of strengthening and rendering more effective and profitable the ancient friendship which has existed between their respective kingdoms;

Her Majesty Queen Victoria having appointed as her Special Envoy and Representative to His Majesty the Emperor Menelek II, James Rennell Rodd,

* English version. The Amharic version signed by King Menelek appeared in the left column of the original Treaty.

Esq., Companion of the Most Distinguished Order of St. Michael and St. George, whose full powers have been found in due and proper form, and His Majesty the Emperor Menelek, negotiating in his own name as King of Kings of Ethiopia, they have agreed upon and do conclude the following Articles, which shall be binding on themselves, their heirs and successors:–

Article I

The subjects of or persons protected by each of the Contracting Parties shall have full liberty to come and go and engage in commerce in the territories of the other, enjoying the protection of the Government within whose jurisdiction they are; but it is forbidden for armed bands from either side to cross the frontier of the other on any pretext whatever without previous authorization from the competent authorities.

Article II

The frontiers of the British Protectorate on the Somali Coast recognized by the Emperor Menelek shall be determined subsequently by exchange of notes between James Rennell Rodd, Esq., as Representative of Her Majesty the Queen, and Ras Maconen, as Representative of His Majesty the Emperor Menelek, at Harrar. These notes shall be annexed to the present Treaty, of which they will form an integral part, so soon as they have received the approval of the High Contracting Parties, pending which the *status quo* shall be maintained.

Article III

The caravan route between Zeyla and Harrar by way of Gildessa shall remain open throughout its whole extent to the commerce of both nations.

Article IV

His Majesty the Emperor of Ethiopia, on the one hand, accords to Great Britain and her Colonies, in respect of import duties and local taxation, every advantage which he may accord to the subjects of other nations.

On the other hand, all material destined exclusively for the service of the Ethiopian State shall, on application from His Majesty the Emperor, be allowed to pass through the port of Zeyla into Ethiopia free of duty.

Article V

The transit of fire-arms and ammunition destined for His Majesty the Emperor of Ethiopia through the territories depending on the Government of Her Britannic Majesty is authorized, subject to the conditions prescribed by the General Act of the Brussels Conference, signed the 2nd July, 1890.

Article VI

His Majesty the Emperor Menelek II, King of Kings of Ethiopia, engages himself towards the Government of Her Britannic Majesty to do all in his power to prevent the passage through his dominions of arms and ammunition to the Mahdists, whom he declares to be the enemies of his Empire.

The present Treaty shall come into force as soon as its ratification by Her Britannic Majesty shall have been notified to the Emperor of Ethiopia, but it is understood that the prescriptions of Article VI shall be put into force from the date of its signature.

In faith of which His Majesty Menelek II, King of Kings of Ethiopia, in his own name, and James Rennell Rodd, Esq., on behalf of Her Majesty Victoria, Queen of Great Britain and Ireland, Empress of India, have signed the present Treaty, in duplicate, written in the English and Amharic languages identically, both texts being considered as official, and have thereto affixed their seals.

Done at Adis Abbaba, the 14th Day of May, 1897.

(L.S.)   (Signed)   JAMES RENNELL RODD.

                            (Seal of His Majesty the Emperor Menelek II)

Annexes to Treaty signed at Adis Abbaba on the
14th May, 1897, by His Majesty the Emperor
Menelek, and by Mr. James Rennell Rodd.

Annex 1

Mr. Rodd to the Emperor Menelek

                                    Adis Abbaba, May 14, 1897.

Your Majesty,
With reference to Article II of the Treaty which we are to sign to-day, I am instructed by my Government, in the event of a possible occupation by Ethiopia of territories inhabited by tribes who have formerly accepted and enjoyed British protection in the districts excluded from the limits of the British Protectorate on the Somali Coast, as recognised by your Majesty, to bring to your knowledge the desire of Her Majesty the Queen to receive from your Majesty an assurance that it will be your special care that these tribes receive equitable treatment, and are thus no losers by this transfer of suzerainty.

In expressing the hope that your Majesty will enable me to give this assurance, I have, &c.

                             [Signed]   RENNELL RODD.

The Emperor Menelek to Mr Rodd

[Translation]

The Conquering Lion of the Tribe of Judah, Menelek II, by the grace of God, King of Kings of Ethiopia, to Mr. Rennell Rodd, Envoy of the Kingdom of England.

Peace be unto you.

YOUR letter, written in Genbot 1889, respecting the Somalis, has reached me. With regard to the question you have put to me, I give you the assurance that the Somalis who may by boundary arrangements become subjects of Ethiopia shall be well treated and have orderly government.

Written at Adis Abbaba, the 6th Genbot, 1889 (14th May, 1897).

[Seal of His Majesty the Emperor Menelek II.]

Annex 2

The Emperor Menelek to Mr. Rodd

[Translation]

From Menelek II, by the grace of God, King of Kings of Ethiopia, Conquering Lion of the tribe of Judah.

May this reach James Rennell Rodd.

Peace be unto you.

WITH reference to the Treaty which we have written in the Amharic and English languages at Adis Abbaba, as I have no interpreter with me who understands the English language well enough to compare the English and Amharic version, if by any possibility in the future there should ever be found any misunderstanding between the Amharic and English versions in any of the Articles of this Treaty, let this translation, which is written in the French language, and which I inclose in this letter, be the witness between us, and if you accept this proposal, send me word of your acceptance by letter.

Dated 7th Genbot, 1889 (14th May, 1897)

[Seal of His Majesty the Emperor Menelek II]

Mr. Rodd to the Emperor Menelek

Adis Abbaba, May 14, 1897.

Your Majesty,

I HAVE the honour to acknowledge the receipt of your Majesty's letter inclosing the French translation of the Treaty which we are to sign this day in English and Amharic, and I agree, on behalf of my Government, to the proposal of your Majesty, that, in case a divergency of opinion should arise hereafter as to the correct interpretation to be given either to the English or Amharic text, the French translation, which has been agreed to on both sides as adequate, should be accepted as furnishing a solution of the matter under dispute.

In recording this assurance, I have, &c.

[Signed]   RENNELL RODD.

Annex 3.

Mr. Rodd to Ras Makunan

Harrar, June 4, 1897 (28 Genbot 1889).

Peace be unto you.

AFTER friendly discussion with your Excellency, I have understood that His Majesty the Emperor of Ethiopia will recognize as frontier of the British Protectorate on the Somali Coast the line which, starting from the sea at the point fixed in the Agreement between Great Britain and France on the 9th February, 1888, opposite the wells of Hadou, follows the caravan-road, described in that Agreement, through Abbassouen till it reaches the hill of Somadou. From this point on the road the line is traced by the Saw mountains and the hill of Egu to Moga Medir; from Moga Medir it is traced by Eylinta Kaddo to Arran Arrhe, near the intersection of latitude 44° east of Greenwich with longitude 9° north. From this point a straight line is drawn to the intersection of 47° east of Greenwich with 8° north. From here the line will follow the frontier laid down in the Anglo-Italian Protocol of the 5th May, 1894, until it reaches the sea.

The tribes occupying either side of the line shall have the right to use the grazing-grounds on the other side, but during their migrations it is understood that they shall be subject to the jurisdiction of the territorial authority. Free access to the nearest wells is equally reserved to the tribes occupying either side of the line.

This understanding, in accordance with Article II of the Treaty signed on the 14th May, 1897 (7th Genbot, 1889), by His Majesty the Emperor Menelek and Mr. Rennell Rodd, at Adis Abbaba, must be approved by the two High Contracting Parties.

I have, &c.

[Signed]   RENNELL RODD

Ras Makunan to Mr. Rodd

[Translation]

Sent from Ras Makunan, Governor of Harrar and its dependencies:

May this reach the Honourable Mr. Rennell Rodd Envoy of the British Kingdom.

I INFORM you to-day that, after long friendly discussion, the boundary of the British Somali Protectorate upon which we have agreed is as follows:--

Starting from the sea-shore opposite the wells of Hadou (as on which the French and the English Governments agreed in February 1888), it follows the caravan-road by Abbassouen till Mount Somadou; from Mount Somadou to Mount Saw; from Mount Saw to Mount Egu; from Mount Egu to Moga Medir; starting from Moga Medir it goes in a direct line to Eylinta Kaddo and Arran Arrhe on 44° east of Greenwich and 9° north, and again in a direct line until 47° east and 8° north. After this the boundary follows the line on which the English and the Italians agreed on the 5th May, 1894, until the sea.

The subjects of both the Contracting Parties are at liberty to cross their frontiers and graze their cattle, but these people, in every place where they go, must obey the Governor of the country in which they are, and the wells which are in the neighbourhood shall remain open for the two parties.

These two letters on which we have agreed, according to Article II of the Treaty of His Majesty the Emperor of Ethiopia and Mr. Rennell Rodd of the 7th Genbot, 1889 (14th May, 1897), the two Sovereigns having seen them, if they approve them shall be sealed again (ratified).

Written at Harrar, the 28th Genbot, 1889 (4th June, 1897).

[Signed]   RAS MAKUNAN.

Mr. Rodd to the Emperor Menelek II.

Cairo, August 30th 1897

From Mr. Rennell Rodd, Special Envoy of Her Majesty Queen Victoria, to His Majesty Menelek II, by the grace of God, King of Kings of Ethiopia.

Peace be unto your Majesty.

I HAVE the honour to annouce that The Queen, my gracious Sovereign, has been pleased to approve and ratify the Treaty which I had the honour to sign with your Majesty on the 14th May last.

Her Majesty has also been pleased to approve of the arrangement which, in accordance with the terms of Article II of the Treaty, was agreed upon between Ras Makunan, as Representative of your Majesty, and myself by exchange of notes relative to the frontier of the British Protectorate in the Somali Coast; and it is presumed by Her Majesty's Government that your Majesty has also approved of it, as they have received no notification to the contrary.

The notes exchanged have accordingly been annexed to the Treaty which has received ratification, signifying Her Majesty's approval of all these documents.

I have now the honour to return herewith the copy of the Treaty intrusted to me by your Majesty, with its ratification in due form.

When I shall have received from your Majesty a letter signifying that this Treaty, thus ratified and approved, has come safely to your Majesty's hands, it will be made public by the Government of the Queen, that all her subjects may observe it and abide by it, and that it may strengthen the ties of friendship between our countries, and increase the feelings of esteem and good-will towards your Majesty which the reception of the British Mission in Ethiopia has awakened in my country.

I pray that your Majesty's life and health may long be preserved, and that your people may have peace and prosperity.

[Signed]   RENNELL RODD

The Emperor Menelek to The Queen

[Translation]

Menelek II, Elect of God, King of Kings of Ethiopia, to Her Most Gracious Majesty Queen Victoria, Queen of Great Britain and Ireland, and Empress of India, Upholder and Keeper of the Christian Religion.

May peace be unto you.

YOUR Majesty's letters of the 28th Hamlé (3rd August) and 22nd (23rd) Mascarem (1st (2nd) October), 1897, and the Treaty with the Great Seal, dated the 28th Hamlé (3rd August), 1897, have reached me, and We received it with joy. The Treaty of Peace which is now between your Government and our Government. We hope it will ever increase in firmness and last for ever.

We ask God to give your Majesty health, and to your kingdom quietness and peace.

Written at Adis Abbaba, the 8th December, 1897, AD.

[Seal of His Majesty the Emperor Menelek II]

III. AGREEMENT BETWEEN GREAT BRITAIN AND ITALY, RESPECTING THE BENADIR COAST AND JURISDICTION IN ZANZIBAR, LONDON 13 JANUARY 1905.

No. 1 [only]

The Marquess of Lansdowne to Signor Pansa.
Foreign Office, January 13th, 1905.

Your Excellency,

In pursuance of previous communications on the subject of an accord between the Zanzibar Government of His Majesty the King of Italy for the purchase by the Italian Government of all the sovereign and other rights of His Highness the Sultan of Zanzibar over the towns, ports, and territory of the Benadir Coast, of which the Administration is now vested in the Italian Government under the Agreement dated the 12th August, 1892, as amended by the Additional Article dated the 1st September, 1896, I have now the honour to propose to your Excellency in the name of the Government of His Highness the Sultan of Zanzibar and on behalf of His Majesty's Government, the following terms of Agreement:–

Purchase by Italy of Benadir Coast

I. The Italian Government will pay to the Government of Zanzibar the sum of 144,000 *l*. This sum, or its sterling equivalent, shall be lodged in the Bank of England to the credit of the Zanzibar Government within three months of the exchange of Notes recording the Agreement.

The rent now payable by the Italian Government shall continue to be paid up to the day on which the purchase money is paid into the Bank.

On the payment of the above-mentioned sum, all rights specially reserved to His Highness the Sultan under the Agreements of 1892 and 1896 shall cease and determine. All subjects of His Britannic Majesty and other British-protected persons, and all subjects of His Highness the Sultan of Zanzibar, shall continue to enjoy in the towns, ports, and territory in question all the privileges and advantages with respect to commerce and shipping which are, or may be, accorded to the subjects of the most favoured nation.

Abandonment by Italy of Ex-territorial Rights in Zanzibar

II. On the same day on which the arrangement indicated in (I) comes into force, all the rights of extra-territoriality now enjoyed by Italy under Treaty, Agreement, or usage, in the dominions of His Highness the Sultan of Zanzibar, shall absolutely cease and determine; and on and after that date the extra-territorial jurisdiction hitherto exercised by His Majesty the King of Italy in His Highness's dominions shall be transferred to His Britannic Majesty's Court for Zanzibar, as constituted under 'The Zanzibar Order in Council, 1897.'

British Right of Pre-emption, Benadir Coast

III. The Italian Government undertake that if at any time Italy should desire to give up the towns, ports, and territory in question, Great Britain shall have the right of pre-emption.

I beg your Excellency to do me the honour to inform me whether the Italian Government consent to these terms of Agreement.

I have, &c.,
LANSDOWNE.

IV. CONVENTION BETWEEN ETHIOPIA AND ITALY SETTLING THE FRONTIER BETWEEN THE ITALIAN POSSESSIONS OF SOMALIA AND THE ETHIOPIAN EMPIRE. – SIGNED AT ADIS ABABA, MAY 16, 1908

[Sanctioned by Royal Italian Decree of July 17, 1908]

[Translation].

His Majesty King Victor Emmanuel III of Italy, in his own name and in the name of his successors, by means of his representative in Adis Ababa, Cavaliere Giuseppe Colli di Felizzano, Captain of Cavalry, and His Majesty

Menelek II, King of Kings of Ethiopia, in his own name and that of his successors, desiring to settle definitively the frontier between the Italian possessions of Somalia and the provinces of the Ethiopian Empire, have determined to sign the following Convention:–

ART. I. The line of frontier between the Italian possessions of Somalia and the provinces of the Ethiopian Empire starts from Dolo at the confluence of the Daua and the Ganale, proceeds eastwards by the sources of the Maidaba and continues as far as the Uebi Scebeli following the territorial boundaries between the tribes of Rahanuin, which remains dependent on Italy, and all the tribes to its north, which remain dependent on Abyssinia.

II. The frontier on the Uebi Scebeli shall be the point where the boundary between the territory of the Baddi-Addi tribe, which remains dependent on Italy, and the territory of the tribes above the Baddi-Addi, which remain dependent on Abyssinia, touches the river.

III. The tribes on the left of the Juba, that of Rahamuin and those on the Uebi Scebeli below the frontier point, shall be dependent on Italy. The tribes of Digodia, of Afgab of Djedjedi and all the others to the north of the frontier line shall be dependent on Abyssinia.

IV. From the Uebi Scebeli the frontier proceeds in a north-easterly direction, following the line accepted by the Italian Government in 1897: all the territory belonging to the tribes towards the coast shall remain dependent on Italy: all the territory of Ogaden and all that of the tribes towards the Ogaden shall remain dependent on Abyssinia.

V. The two Governments undertake to delimit on the spot and as soon as possible the actual line of the frontier as above mentioned.

VI. The two Governments formally undertake not to exercise any interference beyond the frontier line, and not to allow the tribes dependent on them to cross the frontier in order to commit acts of violence to the detriment of the tribes on the other side of the line; but should questions or incidents arise between or on account of the limitrophe tribes, the two Governments shall settle them by common accord.

VII. The two Governments mutually undertake to take no action and to allow their dependents to take no action which may give rise to questions or incidents or disturb the tranquillity of the frontier tribes.

VIII. The present Convention shall, as regards Italy, be submitted to the approval of the Parliament and ratified by His Majesty the King.

Done in duplicate and in identic terms in the two languages, Italian and Amharic.

One copy remains in the hands of the Italian Government, and the other in the hands of the Ethiopian Government.

Given in the city of Adis Ababa, the 16th day of the month of May of the year 1908.

GIUSEPPE COLLI di FELIZZANO
(Seal of Menelek).

Additional act to 16 May convention

[Sanctioned by the King of Italy, with the approval of the Senate and Chamber of Deputies, July 17 1908.]

[Translation]

His Majesty Victor Emmanuel, King of Italy, by means of his representative in Adis Ababa, Cavaliere Giuseppe Colli di Felizzano, Captain of Cavalry, and His Majesty Menelek II, King of Kings of Ethiopia, have agreed on the following Additional Act to the Convention of the 16th May, 1908, for the delimitation of the frontier between the Italian possessions in Somalia and the provinces of the Ethiopian Empire:

Single Article. The Government of His Majesty the King of Italy shall, after approval has been given by the Italian Parliament and ratification by His Majesty the King of the present Additional Act, put at the disposition of His Majesty Menelek II, King of Kings of Ethiopia, the sum of 3,000,000 Italian Lire.

The present Additional Act has been written in duplicate in each of the two languages, Italian and Amharic.

Given in the city of Adis Ababa, the 16th day of the month of May, of the year 1908.

GIUSEPPE COLLI di FELIZZANO
(Seal of Menelek).

Appendix 13

LETTER, DATED 1 MARCH 1950, RECEIVED BY THE
PRESIDENT OF THE TRUSTEESHIP COUNCIL FROM THE
PERMANENT UNITED KINGDOM REPRESENTATIVE ON
THE COUNCIL

[Original text: English]   [2 March 1950]

On 26 January, I gave an undertaking on behalf of His Majesty's Government in the United Kingdom of Great Britain and Northern Ireland that I would furnish the Trusteeship Council with information regarding the provisional line up to which His Majesty's Government proposed that the Italian Government should take over the administration of the Trust Territory of Somaliland.

The details of this provisional line are set out in the enclosure of this letter. It has always been the hope of His Majesty's Government that the question of the provisional frontier between Ethiopia and the Trust Territory of Somaliland would be settled by direct and friendly agreement between the two parties principally concerned – namely, Ethiopia and Italy, as the Authority to which the administration of Somaliland has been entrusted. As members of the Council may be aware, the hopes of His Majesty's Government in this respect have not been fulfilled and it has therefore had no alternative but to make arrangements which, after full consideration, seem to it to represent the maximum degree of administrative convenience for both parties which is practicable in all the circumstances. It must, however, be understood that this arrangement is a provisional one only and without prejudice to the final settlement of this question. I must inform you that the Italian and Ethiopian Governments have been informed of this arrangement by His Majesty's Government.

It is the sincere hope of His Majesty's Government which has been responsible for administering the territory for the past nine years, that the provisional arrangements which it has been obliged to make will work to the satisfaction of the Italian and Ethiopian Administrations. His Majesty's Government also hopes that, pending the final delimitation of the frontier, both parties will make every effort to maintain peace and tranquillity in the area.

I should be grateful if you would arrange for copies of this letter and of the enclosure to be circulated to members of the Council.

[Signed] Alan BURNS

Note

The proposed frontier line is the line shown upon British maps of 1946: East Africa: 1/500,000. GSGS 4355: sheets: NB 38/4, 3rd edition: NB 38/5, 3rd edition: NB 38/3, 2nd edition.

It is defined as follows: From the inter-section of 48 degrees east longitude and of 8 degrees north latitude, thence south-west to a point six kilometres to the south-east of Gherou, thence 3 kilometres to the south of Balli Abdi Ali, thence between Dabarueine and Gheligir, thence to Ferfer leaving Ferfer to the Ethiopian Administration, thence to a locality designated as Casiagur, thence approximately due west between El Garasle and Dudum Har, thence between El Durrei and El Meghet to Bag Berde, leaving Bag Berde to the Ethiopian Administration, thence in a west-south-west direction to south of El Candar to Bur Nohle, through Bur Udalei, thence to the south of Dal Dal Gaandelei, to Uacsen, thence to Iet, leaving Iet to the Italian Administration, thence in a south-south-west direction between Abdi Nur and El Garap, thence between Ber Curale and Sanca Bissach, to a point 3 kilometres north of Laaz Chi Rahanuin, thence between Did Anan and El Did Anan, thence 3 kilometres to the north of Ega Dale, and thence to Dolo. At Dolo, the line follows the already demarcated frontier dividing the locality between Ethiopia and Somaliland.

Appendix 14

GENERAL ASSEMBLY RESOLUTION 1514 (XV) OF 14 DECEMBER 1960 DECLARATION ON THE GRANTING OF INDEPENDENCE TO COLONIAL COUNTRIES AND PEOPLES

The General Assembly

Mindful of the determination proclaimed by the peoples of the world in the Charter of the United Nations to reaffirm faith in fundamental human rights, in the dignity and worth of the human person, in the equal rights of men and women and of nations large and small and to promote social progress and better standards of life in larger freedom,

Conscious of the need for the creation of conditions of stability and well-being and peaceful and friendly relations based on respect for the principles of equal rights and self-determination of all peoples, and of universal respect for, and observance of, human rights and fundamental freedoms for all without distinction as to race, sex, language or religion,

Recognising the passionate yearning for freedom in all dependent peoples and the decisive role of such peoples in the attainment of their independence,

Aware of the increasing conflicts resulting from the denial of or impediments in the way of the freedom of such peoples, which constitutes a serious threat to world peace,

Considering the important role of the United Nations in assisting the movement for independence in Trust and Non-Self-Governing Territories,

Recognising that the peoples of the world ardently desire the end of colonialism in all its manifestations,

Convinced that the continued existence of colonialism prevents the development of international economic co-operation, impedes the social, cultural and economic development of independent peoples and militates against the United Nations ideal of universal peace,

Affirming that peoples may, for their own ends, freely dispose of their natural wealth and resources without prejudice to any obligations arising out of international economic co-operation, based upon the principle of mutual benefit, and international law,

Believing that the process of liberation is irresistible and irreversible and that, in order to avoid serious crises, an end must be put to colonialism and all practices of segregation and discrimination associated therewith,

Welcoming the emergence in recent years of a large number of dependent territories into freedom and independence, and recognising the increasingly powerful trends towards freedom in such territories which have not yet attained independence,

Convinced that all peoples have an inalienable right to complete freedom, the exercise of their sovereignty and the integrity of their national territory,

Solemnly proclaims the necessity of bringing to a speedy and unconditional end colonialism in all its forms and manifestations;

And to this end

Declares that:

1. The subjection of peoples to alien subjugation, domination and exploitation constitutes a denial of fundamental human rights, is contrary to the Charter of the United Nations and is an impediment to the promotion of world peace and co-operation.

2. All peoples have the right to self-determination; by virtue of the right they freely determine their political status and freely pursue their economic, social and cultural development.

3. Inadequacy of political, economic, social or educational preparedness should never serve as a pretext for delaying independence.

4. All armed action or repressive measure of all kinds directed against dependent peoples shall cease in order to enable them to exercise peacefully and freely their right to complete independence, and the integrity of their national territory shall be respected.

5. Immediate steps shall be taken, in Trust and Non-Self-Governing Territories or all other territories which have not yet attained independence, to transfer all powers to the peoples of these territories, without any conditions or reservations, in accordance with their freely expressed will and desire, without any distinction as to race, creed or colour, in order to enable them to enjoy complete independence and freedom.

6. Any attempt aimed at the partial or total disruption of the national unity and the territorial integrity of a country is incompatible with the purposes and principles of the Charter of the United Nations.

7. All States shall observe faithfully and strictly the provisions of the Charter of the United Nations, the Universal Declaration of Human Rights and the present Declaration on the basis of equality, non-interference in the internal affairs of all States, and respect for the sovereign rights of all peoples and their territorial integrity.

Appendix 15

GENERAL ASSEMBLY RESOLUTION 1541 (XV)
ANNEX. PRINCIPLES WHICH SHOULD GUIDE MEMBERS
IN DETERMINING WHETHER OR NOT AN OBLIGATION
EXISTS TO TRANSMIT THE INFORMATION CALLED
FOR IN ARTICLE 73(e) OF THE CHARTER OF
THE UNITED NATIONS.

Principle I

The authors of the Charter of the United Nations had in mind that Chapter XI should be applicable to territories which were then known to be of the colonial type. An obligation exists to transmit information under Article 73(e) of the Charter in respect of such territories whose peoples have not yet attained a full measure of self-government.

Principle II

Chapter XI of the Charter embodies the concept of Non-Self-Governing Territories in a dynamic state of evolution and progress towards a 'full measure of self-government'. As soon as a territory and its peoples attain a full measure of self-government, the obligation ceases. Until this comes about, the obligation to transmit information under Article 73(e) continues.

Principle III

The obligation to transmit information under Article 73(e) of the Charter constitutes an international obligation and should be carried out with due regard to the fulfilment of international law.

Principle IV

Prima facie there is an obligation to transmit information in respect of a territory which is geographically separate and is distinct ethnically and/or culturally from the country administering it.

Principle V

Once it has been established that such a *prima facie* case of geographical and ethnical or cultural distinctness of a territory exists, other elements may then be brought into consideration. These additional elements may be, *inter alia*, of an administrative, political, juridical, economic or historical nature. If they affect the relationship between the metropolitan State and the territory concerned in a manner which arbitrarily places the latter in a position or status of subordination, they support the presumption that there is an obligation to transmit information under Article 73(e) of the Charter.

Principle VI

A Non-Self-Governing Territory can be said to have reached a full measure of self-government by:
(a) Emergence as a sovereign independent state;
(b) Free association with an independent state; or
(c) Integration with an independent state.

Principle VII

(a) Free association should be the result of a free and voluntary choice by the peoples of the territory concerned expressed through informed and democratic processes. It should be one which respects the individuality and the cultural characteristics of the territory and its peoples, and retains for the peoples of the territory which is associated with an independent state the freedom to modify the status of that territory through the expression of their will by democratic means and through constitutional processes.

(b) The associated territory should have the right to determine its internal constitution without outside interference, in accordance with due constitutional processes and the freely expressed wishes of the people. This does not preclude consultations as appropriate or necessary under the terms of the free association agreed upon.

Principle VIII

Integration with an independent State should be on the basis of complete equality between the peoples of the erstwhile Non-Self-Governing Territory and those of the independent country with which it is integrated. The peoples of both territories should have equal status and rights of citizenship and equal guarantees of fundamental rights and freedoms without any distinction or discrimination; both should have equal rights and opportunities for representation and effective participation at all levels in the executive, legislative and judicial organs of government.

Principle IX

Integration should have come about in the following circumstances:

(a) The integrating territory should have attained an advanced stage of self-government with free political institutions, so that its people would have the capacity to make a responsible choice through informed and democratic processes;

(b) The integration should be the result of the freely expressed wishes of the territory's peoples acting with full knowledge of the change in their status, their wishes having been expressed through informed and democratic processes, impartially conducted and based on universal adult suffrage. The United Nations could, when it deems it necessary, supervise these processes.

Principle X

The transmission of information in respect of Non-Self-Governing Territories under Article 73(e) of the Charter is subject to such limitation as security and constitutional considerations may require. This means that the extent of the information may be limited in certain circumstances, but the limitation in Article 73(e) cannot relieve a Member State of the obligations of Chapter XI. The 'limitation' can relate only to the quantum of information of economic, social and educational nature to be transmitted.

Principle XI

The only constitutional considerations to which Article 73(e) of the Charter refers are those arising from constitutional relations of the territory with the Administering Member. They refer to a situation in which the constitution of the territory gives its self-government in economic, social and educational matters through freely elected institutions. Nevertheless, the responsibility for transmitting information under Article 73(e) continues, unless these constitutional relations preclude the Government of Parliament of the Administering Member from receiving statistical and other information of a technical nature relating to economic, social and educational conditions in the territory.

Principle XII

Security considerations have not been invoked in the past. Only in very exceptional circumstances can information on economic, social and educational conditions have any security aspect. In other circumstances, therefore, there should be no necessity to limit the transmission of information on security grounds.

Appendix 16

GENERAL ASSEMBLY RESOLUTION 2625 (XXV). DECLARATION OF PRINCIPLES OF INTERNATIONAL LAW CONCERNING FRIENDLY RELATIONS AND CO-OPERATION AMONG STATES IN ACCORDANCE WITH THE CHARTER OF THE U.N.

The Principle of Equal Rights and Self-Determination of Peoples

By virtue of the principle of equal rights and self-determination of peoples enshrined in the Charter, all peoples have the right freely to determine, without external interference, their political status and to pursue their economic, social and cultural development, and every State has the duty to respect this right in accordance with the provisions of the Charter.

Every State has the duty to promote, through joint and separate action, the realisation of the principle of equal rights and self-determination of peoples, in accordance with the provisions of the Charter, and to render assistance to the United Nations in carrying out the responsibilities entrusted to it by the Charter regarding the implementation of the principle in order:

(a) To promote friendly relations and co-operation among States; and
(b) To bring a speedy end to colonialism, having due regard to the freely expressed will of the peoples concerned;

and bearing in mind that subjection of peoples to alien subjugation, domination and exploitation constitutes a violation of the principle, as well as a denial of fundamental human rights, and is contrary to the Charter of the United Nations.

Every State has the duty to promote through joint and separate action universal respect for and observance of human rights and fundamental freedoms in accordance with the Charter.

The establishment of a sovereign and independent State, the free association or integration with an independent State or the emergence into any other political status freely determined by a people constitute modes of implementing the right of self-determination by that people.

Every State has the duty to refrain from any forcible action which deprives peoples referred to above in the elaboration of the present principle of their right to self-determination and freedom and independence. In their actions against resistance to such forcible action in pursuit of the exercise of their right to self-determination, such peoples are entitled to seek and to receive support in accordance with the purposes and principles of the Charter of the United Nations.

The territory of a colony or other non-self-governing territory has, under the Charter of the United Nations, a status separate and distinct from the territory of the State administering it; and such separate and distinct status under the Charter shall exist until the people of the colony or non-self-governing territory have exercised their right of self-determination in accordance with the Charter, and particularly its purposes and principles.

Nothing in the foregoing paragraphs shall be construed as authorising or encouraging any action which would dismember or impair, totally or in part, the territorial integrity or political unity of sovereign and independent States conducting themselves in compliance with the principle of equal rights and self-determination of peoples as described above and thus possessed of a government representing the whole people belonging to the territory without distinction as to race, creed or colour.

Every State shall refrain from any action aimed at the partial or total disruption of the national unity and territorial integrity of any other State or country.

Appendix 17

WESTERN SAHARA: ADVISORY OPINION OF 16 OCTOBER 1975, PARAS. 48-59.

48. The Court has been asked to state that it ought not to examine the substance of the present request, since the reply to the questions put to it would be devoid of purpose. Spain considers that the United Nations has already affirmed the nature of the decolonization process applicable to Western Sahara in accordance with General Assembly resolution 1514(XV); that the method of decolonization – a consultation of the indigenous population by means of a referendum to be conducted by the administering Power under United Nations auspices – has been settled by the General Assembly. According to Spain, the questions put to the Court are therefore irrelevant, and the answers cannot have any practical effect.

49. Morocco has expressed the view that the General Assembly has not finally settled the principles and techniques to be followed, being free to choose from a wide range of solutions in the light of two basic principles: that of self-determination indicated in paragraph 2 of resolution 1514(XV), and the principle of the national unity and territorial integrity of countries, enunciated in paragraph 6 of the same resolution. Morocco points out that decolonization may come about through the reintegration of a province with the mother country from which it was detached in the process of colonization. Thus, in the view of Morocco, the questions are relevant because the Court's answer will place the General Assembly in a better position to choose the process best suited for the decolonization of the territory.

50. Mauritania maintains that the principle of self-determination cannot be dissociated from that of respect for national unity and territorial integrity; that the General Assembly examines each question in the context of the situations to be regulated; in several instances, it has been induced to give priority to territorial integrity, particularly in situations where the territory had been created by a colonizing Power to the detriment of a State or country to which the territory belonged. Mauritania, pointing out that resolutions 1514(XV) and 2625(XXV) have laid down various methods and possibilities for decolonization, considers, in view of the foregoing, that the questions put to the Court are relevant and should be answered.

51. Algeria states that the self-determination of peoples is the fundamental principle governing decolonization, enshrined in Articles 1 and 55 of the Charter and in General Assembly resolution 1514(XV); that, through successive

resolutions which recommend that the population should be consulted as to its own future, the General Assembly has recognized the right of the people of Western Sahara to exercise free and genuine self-determination; and that the application of self-determination in the framework of such consultation has been accepted by the administering Power and supported by regional institutions and international conferences, as well as endorsed by the countries of the area. In the light of these considerations, Algeria is of the view that the Court should answer the request and, in doing so, should not disregard the fact that the General Assembly, in resolution 3292(XXIX), has itself confirmed its will to apply resolution 1514(XV), that is to say, a system of decolonization based on the self-determination of the people of Western Sahara.

52. Extensive argument and divergent views have been presented to the Court as to how, and in what form, the principles of decolonization apply in this instance, in the light of the various General Assembly resolutions on decolonization in general and on decolonization of the territory of Western Sahara in particular. This matter is not directly the subject of the questions put to the Court, but it is raised as a basis for an objection to the Court's replying to the request. In any event, the applicable principles of decolonization call for examination by the Court, in that they are an essential part of the framework of the questions contained in the request. The reference in those questions to a historical period cannot be understood to fetter or hamper the Court in the discharge of its judicial functions. That would not be consistent with the Court's judicial character; for in the exercise of its functions it is necessarily called upon to take into account existing rules of international law which are directly connected with the terms of the request and indispensable for the proper interpretation and understanding of its Opinion (cf. *I.C.J. Reports* 1962, p. 157).

53. The proposition that those questions are academic and legally irrelevant is intimately connected with their object, the determination of which requires the Court to consider, not only the whole text of resolution 3292(XXIX), but also the general background and the circumstances which led to its adoption. This is so because resolution 3292(XXIX) is the latest of along serious of General Assembly resolutions dealing with Western Sahara. All these resolutions, including resolution 3292(XXIX), were drawn up in the general context of the policies of the General Assembly regarding the decolonization of non-self-governing territories. Consequently, in order to appraise the correctness or otherwise of Spain's view as to the object of the questions posed, it is necessary to recall briefly the basic principles governing the decolonization policy of the General Assembly, the general lines of previous General Assembly resolutions on the question of Western Sahara, and the preparatory work and context of resolution 3292(XXIX).

*

54. The Charter of the United Nations, in Article 1, paragraph 2, indicates, as one of the purposes of the United Nations: 'To develop friendly relations among nations based on respect for the principle of equal rights and self-deter-

mination of peoples . . . ' This purpose is further developed in Articles 55 and 56 of the Charter. Those provisions have direct and particular relevance for non-self-governing territories, which are dealt with in Chapter XI of the Charter. As the Court stated in its Advisory Opinion of 21 June 1971 on *The Legal Consequences for States of the Continued Presence of South Africa in Namibia (South West Africa) notwithstanding Security Council Resolution 276(1970):*

' . . . the subsequent development of international law in regard to non-self-governing territories, as enshrined in the Charter of the United Nations, made the principle of self-determination applicable to all of them.' *(I.C.J. Reports 1971, p. 31)*

55. The principle of self-determination as a right of peoples, and its application for the purpose of bringing all colonial situations to a speedy end, were enunciated in the Declaration on the Granting of Independence to Colonial Countries and Peoples, General Assembly resolution 1514(XV). In this resolution the General Assembly proclaims 'the necessity of bringing to a speedy and unconditional end colonialism in all its forms and manifestations.' To this end the resolution provides *inter alia*:

2. All peoples have the right to self-determination; by virtue of that right they freely determine their political status and freely pursue their economic, social and cultural development. . . .
5. Immediate steps shall be taken, in Trust and Non-Self-Governing Territories or all other territories which have not yet attained independence, to transfer all powers to the peoples of those territories without any conditions or reservations, in accordance with their freely expressed will and desire, without any distinction as to race, creed or colour, in order to enable them to enjoy complete independence and freedom.
6. Any attempt aimed at the partial or total disruption of the national unity and the territorial integrity of a country is incompatible with the purpose and principles of the Charter of the United Nations.'

The above provisions, in particular paragraph 2, thus confirm and emphasize that the application of the right of self-determination requires a free and genuine expression of the will of the peoples concerned.

56. The Court had occasion to refer to this resolution in the above-mentioned Advisory Opinion of 21 June 1971. Speaking of the development of international law in regard to non-self-governing territories the Court there stated:

'A further important stage in this development was the Declaration on the Granting of Independence to Colonial Countries and Peoples (General Assembly resolution 1514(XV) of 14 December 1960), which embraces all peoples and territories which "have not yet attained independence".' *(I.C.J. Reports 1971, p. 31)*

It went on to state:

' . . . the Court must take into consideration the changes which have occurred in the supervening half-century, and its interpretation cannot remain unaffected by the subsequent development of law, through the Charter of the United Nations and by way of customary law' (ibid.).

The Court then concluded:

'In the domain to which the present proceedings relate, the last fifty years, as indicated above, have brought important developments. These developments leave little doubt that the ultimate objective of the sacred trust was the self-determination and independence of the peoples concerned. In this domain, as elsewhere, the *corpus iuris gentium* has been considerably enriched, and this the Court, if it is faithfully to discharge its functions, may not ignore.' (Ibid., pp. 31 f)

57. General Assembly resolution 1514(XV) provided the basis for the process of decolonization which has resulted since 1960 in the creation of many States which are today Members of the United Nations. It is complemented in certain of its aspects by General Assembly resolution 1514(XV), which has been invoked in the present proceedings. The latter resolution contemplates for non-self-governing territories more than one possibility, namely:
(a) emergence as a sovereign independent State;
(b) free association with an independent State; or
(c) integration with an independent State.
At the same time, certain of its provisions give effect to the essential feature of the right of self-determination as established in resolution 1514(XV). Thus principle VII of resolution 1514(XV) declares that: 'Free association should be the result of a free and voluntary choice by the peoples of the territory concerned expressed through informed and democratic processes.' Again, principle IX of resolution 1514 declares that:

'Integration should have come about in the following circumstances: . . .
(b) The integration should be the result of the freely expressed wishes of the territory's peoples acting with full knowledge of the change in their status, their wishes having been expressed through informed and democratic processes, impartially conducted and based on universal adult suffrage. The United Nations could, when it deems it necessary, supervise these processes.'

58. General Assembly resolution 2625(XXV), 'Declaration on Principles of International Law concerning Friendly Relations and Co-operation among States in accordance with the Charter of the United Nations', – to which reference was also made in the proceedings – mentions other possibilities besides independence, association or integration. But in doing so it reiterates the basic need to take account of the wishes of the people concerned:

'The establishment of a sovereign and independent State, the free association or integration with an independent State or the emergence into any other political status *freely determined by a people* constitute modes of implementing the right of self-determination by that people.'

Resolution 2625(XXV) further provides that:

'Every State has the duty to promote, through joint and separate action, realization of the principle of equal rights and self-determination of peoples in accordance with the provisions of the Charter, and to render assistance to the United Nations in carrying out the responsibilities entrusted to it by the Charter regarded the implementation of the principle, in order: . . .

148

(b) To bring a speedy end to colonialism, having due regard to the freely expressed will of the peoples concerned.'

59. The validity of the principle of self-determination, defined as the need to pay regard to the freely expressed will of peoples, is not affected by the fact that in certain cases the General Assembly has dispensed with the requirement of consulting the inhabitants of a given territory. Those instances were based either on the consideration that a certain population did not constitute a 'people' entitled to self-determination or on the conviction that a consultation was totally unnecessary, in view of special circumstances.

Appendix 18

GENERAL ASSEMBLY RESOLUTION 742(VIII). ANNEX. LIST OF FACTORS INDICATIVE OF THE ATTAINMENT OF INDEPENDENCE OR OF OTHER SEPARATE SYSTEMS OF SELF-GOVERNMENT

First Part. Factors Indicative of the Attainment of Independence

A. INTERNATIONAL STATUS

1. *International responsibility.* Full international responsibility of the Territory for the acts inherent in the exercise of its external sovereignty and for the corresponding acts in the administration of its internal affairs.
2. *Eligibility for membership in the United Nations.*
3. *General international relations.* Power to enter into direct relations of every kind with other governments and with international institutions and to negotiate, sign and ratify international instruments.
4. *National defence.* Sovereign right to provide for its national defence.

B. INTERNAL SELF-GOVERNMENT

1. *Form of government.* Complete freedom of the people of the Territory to choose the form of self-government which they desire.
2. *Territorial government.* Freedom from control of interference by the government of another State in respect of the internal government (legislature, executive, judiciary, and administration of the Territory).
3. *Economic, social and cultural jurisdiction.* Complete autonomy in respect of economic, social and cultural affairs.

Second Part. Factors Indicative of the Attainment of Other Separate Systems of Self-Government

APPENDIX 18

A. GENERAL

1. *Opinion of the population.* The opinion of the population of the Territory, freely expressed by informed and democratic processes, as to the status or change in status which they desire.

2. *Freedom of choice.* Freedom of choosing on the basis of the right of self-determination of peoples between several possibilities, including independence.

3. *Voluntary limitation of sovereignty.* Degree of evidence that the attribute or attributes of sovereignty which are not individually exercised will be collectively exercised by the larger entity thus associated and the freedom of the population of a Territory which has associated itself with the metropolitan country to modify at any time this status through the expression of their will by democratic means.

4. *Geographical considerations.* Extent to which the relations of the Non-Self-Governing Territory with the capital of the metropolitan government may be affected by circumstances arising out of their respective geographical positions, such as separation by land, sea or other natural obstacles; and extent to which the interests of boundary States may be affected, bearing in mind the general principle of good-neighbourliness referred to in Article 74 of the Charter.

5. *Ethnic and cultural considerations.* Extent to which the populations are of different race, language or religion or have a distinct cultural heritage, interests or aspirations, distinguishing them from the peoples of the country with which they freely associate themselves.

6. *Political advancement.* Political advancement of the population sufficient to enable them to decide upon the future destiny of the Territory with due knowledge.

B. INTERNATIONAL STATUS

1. *General international relations.* Degree or extent to which the Territory exercises the power to enter freely into direct relations of every kind with other governments and with international institutions and to negotiate, sign and ratify international instruments freely. Degree or extent to which the metropolitan country is bound, through constitutional provisions or legislative means, by the freely expressed wishes of the Territory in negotiating, signing and ratifying international conventions which may influence conditions in the Territory.

2. *Change of political status.* The right of the metropolitan country or the Territory to change the political status of that Territory in the light of the consideration whether that Territory is or is not subject to any claim or litigation on the part of another State.

3. *Eligibility for membership in the United Nations.*

C. INTERNAL SELF-GOVERNMENT

1. *Territorial government.* Nature and measure of control or interference, if any, by the government of another State in respect of the internal government, for example, in respect of the following:

Legislature: The enactment of laws for the Territory by an indigenous body whether fully elected by free and democratic processes or lawfully constituted in a manner receiving the free consent of the population.

Executive: The selection of members of the executive branch of the government by the competent authority in the Territory receiving consent of the indigenous population, whether that authority is hereditary or elected, having regard also to the nature and measure of control, if any, by an outside agency on that authority, whether directly or indirectly exercised in the constitution and conduct of the executive branch of the government;

Judiciary: The establishment of courts of law and the selection of judges.

2. *Participation of the population.* Effective participation of the population in the government of the Territory: (a) Is there an adequate and appropriate electoral and representative system? (b) Is this electoral system conducted without direct or indirect interference from a foreign government?

3. *Economic, social and cultural jurisdiction.* Degree of autonomy in respect of economic, social and cultural affairs, as illustrated by the degree of freedom from economic pressure as exercised, for example, by a foreign minority group which, by virtue of the help of a foreign Power, has acquired a privileged economic status prejudicial to the general economic interest of the people of the Territory, and by the degree of freedom and lack of discrimination against the indigenous population of the Territory in social legislation and social developments.

Third Part. Factors Indicative of the Free Association of a Territory on Equal Basis with the Metropolitan or other Country as an Integral Part of that Country or in any other Form.

A. GENERAL

1. *Opinion of the Population.* The opinion of the population of the Territory, freely expressed by informed and democratic processes, as to the status or change in status which they desire.

2. *Freedom of choice.* The freedom of the population of a Non-Self-Governing Territory which has associated itself with the metropolitan country as an integral part of that country or in any form to modify this status through the expression of their will by democratic means.

3. *Geographical considerations.* Extent to which the relations of the Territory with the capital of the central government may be affected by circumstances

arising out of their respective geographical positions, such as separation by land, sea or other natural obstacles. The right of the metropolitan country or the Territory to change the political status of that Territory in the light of the consideration whether that Territory is or is not subject to any claim or litigation on the part of another State.

4. *Ethnic and cultural considerations.* Extent to which the population are of difference race, language or religion or have a distinct cultural heritage, interests or aspirations, distinguishing them from the peoples of the country with which they freely associate themselves.

5. *Political advancement.* Political advancement of the population sufficient to enable them to decide upon the future destiny of the Territory with due knowledge.

6. *Constitutional considerations.* Association by virtue of treaty or bilateral agreement affecting the status of the Territory, taking into account (i) whether the constitutional guarantees extend equally to the associated Territory, (ii) whether there are powers in certain matters constitutionally reserved to the Territory or to the central authority, and (iii) whether there is provision for the participation of the Territory on a basis of equality in any changes in the constitutional system of the State.

B. STATUS

1. *Legislative representation.* Representation without discrimination in the central legislative organs on the same basis as other inhabitants and regions.

2. *Participation of the population.* Effective participation of the population in the government of the Territory: (a) Is there an adequate and appropriate electoral and representative system? (b) Is this electoral system conducted without direct or indirect interference from a foreign government?*

---

* For example, the following questions would be relevant:
(i) Has each adult inhabitant equal power (subject to special safeguards for minorities) to determine the character of the government of the Territory?
(ii) Is this power exercised freely, i.e., is there an absence of undue influence over and coercion on the voter and of the imposition of disabilities on particular political parties?
Some tests which can be used in the application of this factor are as follows:
    (a) The existence of effective measures to ensure the democratic expression of the will of the people;
    (b) The existence of more than one political party in the Territory.
    (c) The existence of a secret ballot;
    (d) The existence of legal prohibitions on the exercise of undemocratic practices in the course of elections;
    (e) The existence for the individual elector of a choice between candidates of differing political parties;
    (f) The absence of 'martial law' and similar measures at election times;
(iii) Is each individual free to express his political opinions, to support or oppose any political party or cause, and to criticise the government of the day?

3. *Citizenship*. Citizenship without discrimination on the same basis as other inhabitants.

4. *Government officials*. Eligibility of officials from the Territory to all public offices of the central authority, by appointment or election, on the same basis as those from other parts of the country.

C. INTERNAL CONSTITUTIONAL CONDITIONS

1. *Suffrage*. Universal and equal suffrage, and free periodic elections, characterised by an absence of undue influence over and coercion of the voter or of the imposition of disabilities on particular political parties.†

† For example, the following tests would be relevant:

(a) The existence of effective measures to ensure the democratic expression of the will of the people;

(b) The existence of more than one political party in the Territory;

(c) The existence of a secret ballot;

(d) The existence of legal prohibitions on the exercise of undemocratic practices in the course of elections;

(e) The existence for the individual elector of a choice between candidates of differing political parties;

(f) The absence of 'martial law' and similar measures at election times;

(g) Freedom of each individual to express his political opinions, to support or oppose any political party or cause, and to criticise the government of the day.

Appendix 19

OAU, AHG/RES. 16(I)
GENERAL RESOLUTION ON BORDER DISPUTES
ADOPTED BY THE CONFERENCE OF HEADS OF STATE

The Assembly of Heads of State and Government meeting in its First Ordinary Session in Cairo, UAR, from 17 to 21 July 1964:

Considering that border problems constitute a grave and permanent factor of dissension,

Conscious of the existence of extra-African manoeuvres aimed at dividing African States,

Considering further that the borders of African States, on the day of their independence, constitute a tangible reality,

Recalling the establishment in the course of the Second Ordinary Session of the Council of the Committee of Eleven charged with studying further measures for strengthening African Unity,

Recognizing the imperious necessity of settling, by peaceful means and within a strictly African framework, all disputes between African States,

Recalling further that all Member States have pledged, under Article VI of the Charter of African Unity, to respect scrupulously all principles laid down in paragraph 3 of Article III of the Charter of the Organization of African Unity,

1. *Solemnly reaffirms* the strict respect by all Member States of the Organization for the principles laid down in paragraph 3 of Article III of the Charter of the Organization of African Unity;

2. *Solemnly declares* that all Member States pledge themselves to respect the borders existing on their achievement of national independence.

A Working Chronolgy

1867	Menelik proclaims himself independent King of Shoa
1868-89	Yohannes IV, Emperor of Ethiopia.
1869	Italians purchase Assab. Djibouti replaced Obock as French coaling station.
1871-6	Menelik campaigns against the Wallo Galla tribes.
1874	Yohannes IV appeals for Russian help against Muslims.
1875	Three Egyptian expeditions against Ethiopia. Egyptians defeated near Gura.
1882	Italy established colony of Eritrea.
1883	Mahdi defeats Anglo-Egyptian forces at El Obeid, Sudan. Britain decides to evacuate Sudan.
1884	Gordon reaches Khartoum to evacuate Egyptians. Menelik signs treaty with Britain against Mahdi. Britain establishes British Somaliland protectorate.
1885	Italy occupies Massawa. France occupies Djibouti. Mahdi takes Khartoum – Gordon killed.
1886	Sultan of Harar defeats Italian expedition.
1889	Yohannes IV killed in battle. Menelik proclaims himself emperor.
1891	Menelik denounces Italian claims to a protectorate.
1892	Tafari Makonnen (later Emperor Haile Selassie) born.
1895	Italian troops enter Ethiopia.
1896	Ethiopians defeat Italians at Adowa; Italy forced to sue for peace.
1897	Ethiopia annexes much Somali territory in various expeditions.
1900	
1925	Italy completes occupation of Italian Somaliland under terms of 1889 protectorate.
1928	Italy signs 20 year Treaty of Friendship with Ethiopia. Coup d'état in Ethiopia. Ras Tafari takes control and is crowned Negus by Empress Zawditu.
1930	Ras Gugsa Wolfie, brother of Empress Zawditu, revolts against Negus Tafari and loses. 2 April, Empress Zawditu dies and 3 April, Ras Tafari proclaimed Emperor Haile Selassie.
1970	Ethiopia declares state of emergency in Eritrea.
1973	Somalia joins Arab League.
1974	Haile Şelassie deposed as Emperor of Ethiopia and military assume control. Campaign of terror against opposition.
1977	Fidel Castro and Nikolai Podgorny visit Mogadishu but fail to bring Somalia into Soviet plan. Soviets start supplying arms to Ethiopia.

Cuban advisers start to arrive in Addis Ababa, (May). Djibouti declared independent (June). Soviets stop arms supply to Somalia (July). US offers arms to Somalia but withdraws offer – but Somalia WSLF start offensive in Ogaden. Somalis throw Soviets out of Somalia (November). Soviet build-up of Cubans in Ethiopia accelerates (December).

1978   Somalis withdraw from Ogaden and war ends. Start of massive influx of refugees. Ethiopian start indiscriminate bombing of Somali villages.

1979   Refugees continue to arrive and Ethiopian bombings continue.

1980   Ethiopian bombings continue and Ethiopia temporarily invades Somalia in Dolo region.

1981   Refugees affected first by drought and then by flood. Formation of Libya-Ethiopia-South Yemen alliance.

1982   Ethiopian attack on Eritrea. Official UN figure for refugees given as 700,000 (Feb). Ethiopia invades Somalia at Balam Bale and Galdogob.

1983   Ethiopian troops remain on Somali soil.

1984   Ethiopian bombing of Borama (north Somalia) 37 school-children killed. Continuing Ethiopian air-raids on Somali towns ICARA II (Geneva – 9 to 11 July). New Communist Party foisted on Ethiopia (Sept). Horn of Africa and Aden Council launched in GB – sends fact-finding missions to Sudan and Somalia. Mr. Malcolm Rifkind visits Horn of Africa. European Parliament adopts Resolution on The Horn of Africa. German Horn of Africa Council formed in Bonn, West Germany.

1985   The Horn of Africa and Aden Council changed its name to The British Horn of Africa Council.

Bibliography

The Mad Mullah of Somaliland. D. Jardine, 1923.
The Blue Nile. Alan Moorhead, 1962.
First Footsteps in East Africa. Sir R. Burton, rpt. 1966.
Ethiopia – A New Political History. R. Greenfield, 1965.
A Modern History of Somalia. I.M. Lewis, 1965, 1980.
My Country – My People. Collected speeches of President Siad Barre. Mogadishu, 1973.
The Portion of Somali Territory under Ethiopian Colonisation. Mogadishu, 1974.
Memorandum on Colonisation in French Somaliland. Mogadishu, 1975.
Somalia – Five Years of Revolutionary Progress. Mogadishu, 1974.
Somalia Today. Mogadishu, 1975.
A Legal Analysis of Ethiopia's Occupation of Western Somalia. Mogadishu, 1977.
Objectives and Policy of Resettlement. Mogadishu, 1977.
Beautiful Somalia. Mogadishu, 1978.
Horn of Africa, Vol. 1, No. 3. USA, 1978.
The Disastrous Damages of Ethiopian Aggression. Mogadishu, 1978.
Go from my Country. Mogadishu, 1978.
Washington Review – White Paper – 'The Horn of Africa'. USA, 1978.
Basis of the Conflict in the Horn of Africa. Mogadishu, 1978.
Background to the liberation struggle of Western Somalia. Mogadishu, 1978.
Readers Digest. Vol. 113, No. 678. 10/1978.
East-West Digest. Vol. 14, Nos. 11 and 14. London, 1978.
War in the Horn of Africa. A firsthand report of the challenges for US policy. Official Report to the Committee of International Relations, US House of Representatives. USA, 1978.
March of the Revolution. Mogadishu, 1979.
Somalia's Arab, African and International Role. Mogadishu, 1980.
Speech delivered by President Siad Barre on 21 October 1980. Mogadishu, 1980.
The True Situation in the Horn of Africa and surrounding Region. Mogadishu, 1981.
Somali Culture, History and Social Institutions. I. M. Lewis. London, 1981.
Refugees, UNHCR. Geneva, 1981.
Short and Long Term Programme for Refugees. Mogadishu, 1981.
Hansard official Reports (Lords and Commons), 1978-85.
Conflict in The Horn of Africa. Colin Legum and Bill Lee, 1977.
Self-Determination in Western Somalia. W.M. Reisman, (undated).

Eritrea. David Pool, 1979 and 1982.

The Horn of Africa. James E. Dougherty, 1982.

The Betrayal of the Somalis. Louis FitzGibbon, 1982.

Nationalism and Self-Determination in The Horn of Africa. Edited by I.M. Lewis, 1983.

Conflict and Intervention in The Horn of Africa. Bereket Habte Selassie, 1980.

Ethiopia's Invasion of Somalia 1982-83. Ministry of Foreign Affairs, Mogadishu, 1983.

Ibn Battuta. Routledge and Kegan Paul, 1983.

Counting Quintals. Gayle E. Smith, 1983.

The Red Sea. Arab Research Centre, 1984.

Les Droits de l'Homme et L'Afrique. Benoit S. Ngom, 1984.

The Emperor. Ryszard Kapuscinski, 1984.

Index

Note: Place names in italics, countries excluded. Due to the complexities of the legal references, this Index is limited to main names only and does not include those in the appendices.